Seamus *Heaney*

Seamus Heaney

A Student's Guide to the Selected Poems 1965-75

Nicholas McGuinn

ARNOLD-WHEATON

Arnold-Wheaton
A Division of E.J. Arnold & Son Limited
Parkside Lane, Leeds LS11 5TD

A member of the Pergamon Group
Headington Hill Hall, Oxford OX3 0BW

Copyright © 1986 Nicholas McGuinn

All rights reserved. No part of this publication may be reproduced, stored in a retrieval system, or transmitted, in any form or by any means, electronic, electrostatic, magnetic tape, mechanical, photocopying, recording or otherwise, without permission in writing from the publishers.

First published 1986

Printed in Great Britain by A. Wheaton & Co. Ltd, Hennock Road, Exeter

ISBN 0560–55004–9

To the Reader

Seamus Heaney is a poet who expects a great deal from his audience. Students who are attracted to **Death of a Naturalist** and **Door into the Dark** for their vivid and forthright descriptions of such safely familiar themes as nature, childhood and rural life, often draw back in confusion from his complex later work. This response is understandable. As the poetic lines of **Wintering Out** and **North** grow shorter and more austere, they demand an increasingly sophisticated knowledge of linguistics, history, politics, mythology and literature from the reader.

The glossaries and historical notes placed at the back of this book are designed to make access to the text easier. They should be read with the poems. The main part of the book is divided into four chapters which correspond to the four volumes of verse included in the **Selected Poems**. I have approached the work thematically, trying to show how each volume represents a particular stage in Heaney's development from "nature" to "national" poet. The subheadings are meant to help those students who wish to "dip" into the book and to follow one particular theme through from **Death of a Naturalist** to **North**.

Seamus Heaney does not write in the language of the "rational", materialistic world. Like Ted Hughes and other poets of the post-Christian, post-Holocaust age, his concern is to discover (or rediscover) a myth which will help his people to find peace in their strife-torn society. To follow Heaney on his artistic journey, the reader needs imagination rather than reason – and must look at the world, not through the eyes of St. Patrick, but the older eyes of Oisin.

The latest of the **Selected Poems** are now at least eleven years old. **North** appeared in 1975, and since then Heaney has published two major collections of verse and one long verse translation from the Irish. I hope that this guide will encourage students to explore the poet's later work and to discover more about the tragic history of Ireland which has done so much to shape his poetic vision.

Howden, East Yorkshire. March, 1986

For Rachel

Acknowledgements

The editor and publishers wish to thank the following who have kindly given permission for the use of copyright material:

Faber and Faber Ltd., for the extracts used from the following poems by Seamus Heaney:
Personal Helicon, Blackberry Picking, Death of a Naturalist, Digging, Follower, Churning Day and *At a Potato Digging,* from **Death of a Naturalist** by Seamus Heaney,
Undine, Beyond Sargasso, Thatcher, The Wife's Tale, Lifting, Forge, Up the Shore, The Given Note, Exposure, A Requiem for the Croppies, The Plantation, Shoreline, The God in the Tree, The Peninsula, Bogland, A Lough Neagh Sequence and *At Ardboe Point,* from **Door into the Dark** by Seamus Heaney,
Ministry of Fear, Bog Oak, The Last Mummer, Bye-Child, Servant Boy, Gifts of Rain, Limbo, Summer Home, Nerthus, Serenades, Shore Woman, Stump, Westering, Good-Night, Anahorish, The Other Side and *Traditions,* from **Wintering Out** by Seamus Heaney,
Whatever you say, say nothing, Summer 1961, Act of Union, Bog Queen, The Tollund Man, Punishment, Exposure, Hercules and Antaeus, Strange Fruit, Antaeus, Gifts of Rain, Viking Dublin, Funeral Rites. Sunlight, The Seed Cutters and *Shoreline* from **North** by Seamus Heaney,
for the extracts reprinted from **Preoccupations: Selected Prose 1969-78** by Seamus Heaney, 1980,
for the extract from the article by John Haffenden from **Viewpoints**, 1981,
Seamus Heaney, for the extracts reprinted from his articles in **The Listener**, 1968-1974: *A Poet's Childhood, Celtic Fringe, Viking Fringe, After the Synge Song, Old Derry's Walls, Views, Mother Ireland, Lost Ulsterman, Summoning Lazarus,* and *Seamus Heaney Praises Lough Erne.*
for the extract reprinted from the **New Statesman**, *Out of London: Ulster's Troubles,* 1966,
for the extract from the article in the **Poetry Book Society Bulletin**, the Poetry Book Society, 1975.
Routledge and Kegan Paul P.L.C., for the extract from **Irish Folk Ways** by E. Evans, 1957.
Methuen and Co. Ltd., for the extract from **Modern Ireland** by Alan Dures, 1973.
Ploughshares, for the extract from *An Interview with S. Heaney,* James Randall, 1979.

Oxford University Press, for the extract from Annales *The Oxford Book of Literary Anecdotes* by William Camden, 1975.

C. B. Fox, for the extract from *The Painter's Eye*, **The Spectator**, 1966.

The Honest Ulsterman, for the extract from *Escaped from the Massacre*, **The Honest Ulsterman**, Ciaran Carson, 1975.

Edward Pygge, for the extract from **The Review**, 1970.

Lord Windlesham, for the extract from the article in the **Guardian**, December, 1972.

Monie Begley, for the extract from **Rambles in Ireland**, Devlin-Adair, 1977.

Seamus Deane, for the extract from *Unhappy at Home*, **The Crane Bag**, 1977.

Photographs are reproduced by kind permission of the following:

Royal Danish Embassy: The Tollund Man.

National Museum of Ireland: A trial piece.

Geray Sweeney: Seamus Heaney, Lough Neagh eels, Storing potatoes, and the cover – Lough Neagh.

Note: Every effort has been made to trace the copyright holders of the extracts reprinted in this book. We apologise for any inadvertent omission, which can be rectified in a subsequent reprint.

I would like to thank the students of Beverley and Honley High Schools who explored the poetry of Seamus Heaney with me. I also thank Pam Hutchinson and Andy Whittle for their help.

Contents

To the Reader	5
Acknowledgements	7
Map: Northern Ireland	12
Chapter One: 'Death of a Naturalist'	13
The loss of childhood innocence	14
A sense of guilt	16
Alienation from the family	16
The need for a sense of place	17
Poetry as a weapon	18
The poet as observer	19
Follower	20
Digging	21
Reconciliation	21
The poetic landscape of 'Death of a Naturalist'	22
Language and diction	23
Summary and conclusion	24
Notes and References	25
Chapter Two: 'Door into the Dark'	27
A new sense of confidence	28
Poetic influences	28
Imagery of movement	29
Undine	30
Experiments with metrical form	32
Beyond Sargasso	32
The widening poetic landscape	33
The magical world-view	34
The theme of history	35
The connection between landscape and history	36
Bogland as a poetic metaphor	37
Bogland	37
The search for an Irish myth	38
Landscape interpreted as myth	39
The poet as High Priest	40
History as sacrifice	40
Reconciliation with nature	41
Summary and conclusion	42
Notes and References	44

Map: Ireland	46
A selection of Photographs	47
Seamus Heaney at home	47
The Tollund Man	48
Storing potatoes	49
Lough Neagh eels	50
A trial piece	51
Chapter Three: 'Wintering Out'	53
Political events in Ulster 1963–1972	54
Heaney's response to the situation in Ulster	55
A sense of divided loyalty	57
The poetic landscape of 'Wintering Out'	59
The fatalism of 'Wintering Out'	60
The theme of haunting	62
The themes of love and nature	63
"Befitting emblems of adversity". Heaney's response to the crisis in Ulster in 'Wintering Out'.	64
The inadequacy of Christian emblems	68
The emblem of Tollund Man and the magical world-view of 'Wintering Out'.	69
The theme of language	73
The structure of 'Wintering Out'	75
Summary and conclusion	79
Notes and References	81
Chapter Four: 'North'	83
The Divided Structure of 'North'	84
Heaney's response to the pressures of the Ulster crisis	85
From public to private response: The changed role of the poet in 'North'	87
The *Bog Poems* of 'North'	88
The use of symbolism for self-analysis	92
Hercules against Antaeus: The symbolic figures of 'North'	93
The poet as Hamlet	96
The public poems of 'North': The exploration of the "Irish myth" resumed and concluded	97
Poems of Healing: The return to Mossbawn	101
Heaney's return to his poetic roots	102
Summary and conclusion	105
Notes and References	107

Glossary to 'The Selected Poems'   109

Historical Notes to 'The Selected Poems'   111

At a Potato Digging   111

Shoreline   111

Requiem for the Croppies   111

Bog Oak   112

The Last Mummer   113

The Other Side   113

The Tollund Man   114

Funeral Rites   115

Shoreline, North, Viking Dublin: Trial Pieces   115

Bog Queen   116

The Grauballe Man   116

Punishment, Strange Fruit   116

The Politics of Northern Ireland   118

Political events since 1914   121

Suggestions for further reading   123

Books about Heaney's poetry   123

Books and essays by Seamus Heaney   123

Seamus Heaney: Reference Works   124

Books on the History of Ireland   124

Books about Northern Ireland   125

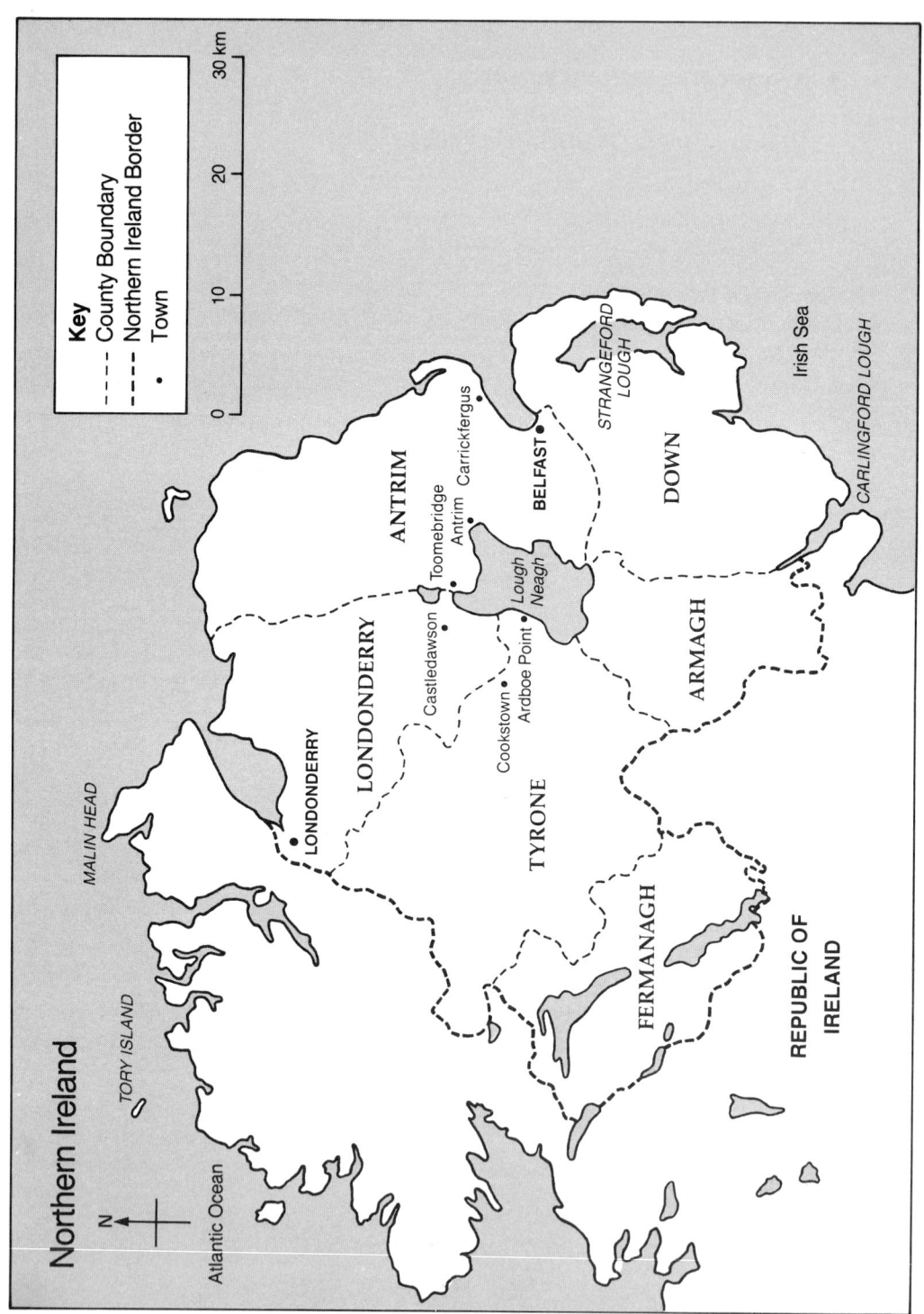

Chapter One

'Death of a Naturalist'

The loss of childhood innocence.

Seamus Heaney's first volume of poetry, **Death of a Naturalist**, was published by Faber and Faber in 1966 when he was 27 years old. The main concern of the collection is the loss of childhood innocence and the gaining of adult experience. The "naturalist" of the title is a child whom English Romantic poets such as Blake and Wordsworth would have recognised. He is a "naturalist" in two senses: first, because he lives in a close relationship with nature, and second, because he acts according to his instincts rather than the rules of society.

Heaney's first book is peopled by such free spirits – prying into roots and fingering slime in *Personal Helicon*, splashing "Delightedly" through "the sucking clabber" in *Poem*. Yet, just as Wordsworth's child lives to see his joyful vision "fade into the light of common day"[1], so Heaney's children experience a moment of intense drama which changes them irrevocably. In *Death of a Naturalist* a "thick ... bass chorus' of "angry frogs" sends the boy running, "sickened", away from the comforting world of Miss Walls forever. In *Mid-Term Break* a father's tearful helplessness in the face of death forces his young son to assume adult responsibility.

Heaney's own childhood was deeply touched by this Wordsworthian sense of vision and fear of loss. Nowhere in his prose works does he write with greater warmth and affection than when describing his early years on the family farm at Mossbawn in County Derry. In the essay entitled *A Poet's Childhood*, for example, the phrase "I love" or "I loved" occurs four times in the course of one page as he tenderly recalls the characters and events of those days. Like the "naturalist" of the poem, the young Heaney had freedom to explore his surroundings with uninhibited delight, dawdling on the way to school to watch waterhens,[2] or plunging naked into a "moss-hole" purely for the pleasure of "treading the liver-thick mud" and coming out "smeared and weedy and darkened."[3]

So closely does Heaney feel bound to the Derry landscape that he describes himself as being "betrothed" to it, and a recurrent theme in his prose writing about childhood is the desire to possess the landscape entirely, to make it permanent and safe, by creating a "secret nest" or "sunlit lair" in "the pea-drills in a field behind the house", the "fork of a beech tree at the head of our lane" or the "top of the dresser". One of his earliest and most abiding memories recalls the breaching of that natural sanctuary by the adult world:

I'm sitting as if just wakened from a winter sleep and gradually become aware of voices, coming closer, calling my name, and for no reason at all I have begun to weep.[4]

By the time the poems in **Death of a Naturalist** were written, Heaney had come to understand the reason for that moment of early sorrow. Like Blake and Wordsworth and poets before them, he is grieving, in this first volume, for what he has called the "fall into manhood"[5]. Try as he might to defend that "secret nest" of childhood, his "small imperfect limits would keep breaking", just as surely as the dams he recalls building in *Poem*, would "burst before the rising autumn rain."

To appear before the public for the first time with a collection of poems about the loss of childhood is an ambitious and risky venture. The new author immediately invites comparison with all the great works of the past which have already explored that theme. Heaney himself has suggested that **Death of a Naturalist** came, not through choice, but because it had to be. "I wrote about childhood", he observed in 1971, "because I couldn't help it".[6] It is as though, in this first book of verse, Heaney is honouring an obligation and freeing himself of a burden. His aim is not so much to analyse those childhood experiences of loss, but to relive them, pay homage to them, and then let them go. Like a film-maker, he "freezes" the last "frame" of a poem at the moment of pained discovery – as the child turns from the flax-dam, for example, or stands before his dead brother's pathetic four-foot coffin. Each final image from, for example, *Death of a Naturalist*, *Blackberry-Picking* and *Mid-Term Break*, enters the public world of the printed page like a ghost entering the daylight. The act of commemoration is also an act of exorcism.

This desire to drive away ghosts from the past, to "set the darkness echoing" as Heaney puts it in *Personal Helicon*, is one of the aims of his first collection of verse. But in that same poem he also declares: "I rhyme/To see myself"; and it is with poetry as "revelation of the self to the self"[7] that he is also deeply concerned here. Viewed in this light, works like *Death of a Naturalist* and *Blackberry-Picking* for example, can be interpreted not simply as lyrical evocations of loss but also as portraits of their author's state of mind.

A sense of guilt

At a first reading, the structure of two verse paragraphs in each poem suggests a simple division between possession and loss, innocence and experience. In the first paragraph, the boy is fascinated by the frogs and enjoys the pleasure of blackberry-picking. In the second, he runs in terror and finds the fruit rotting. However, a closer examination shows that even in the supposedly perfect world described in each first paragraph, there is something wrong. In *Blackberry-Picking*, the berries are portrayed in a grotesquely surreal way which owes more to nightmare than childhood delight: "on top big dark blobs burned/Like a plate of eyes." The flax-dam in *Death of a Naturalist* is no playground paradise but a place of corruption and filth which "festered" like a disease "in the heart/Of the townland".

These strange and negative characteristics are not inherent in blackberries or flax-dams; and the fact that Heaney chooses to describe them in this way suggests that something is distorting his vision of the natural world. Just exactly what is wrong is revealed most clearly in *Death of a Naturalist* where the boy's perception of the frogs is transformed at the moment when, connecting their present "bass chorus" with his earlier theft of frogspawn, he suddenly sees himself as a criminal whom the "great slime kings" have come to punish by demanding nothing less than the death of the naturalist in him. It is a sense of guilt which distorts Heaney's vision of nature; and it is guilt, too, which shapes the structure of *Death of a Naturalist* and *Blackberry-Picking*. The dramatic tension in the two poems is not so much between innocence and experience as between crime and punishment. In both poems the crime is theft; but in this latter poem there is a ritualistic quality to the punishment: why does the boy go to the trouble of hoarding the blackberries every year when he knows each time that he is only storing up disappointment for himself? It is almost as though he feels obliged to make a yearly act of atonement to the natural world.

Alienation from the family

The sense of guilt glimpsed in *Death of a Naturalist* and *Blackberry-Picking* emerges more strongly in Heaney's poems about his family. In *Digging* and *Follower* particularly, the source of that guilt is clearly identified. Both poems praise the family's farming skills – his father's digging and ploughing, his grandfather's turf-cutting – only to draw a contrast between their prowess and the poet's lack of it. The boy who "stumbled" in his father's "hob-nailed wake" grows into the adult who is forced to admit that "I've no spade to follow men like them." What has come between father and son here is first of all, education, and secondly and more ironically the very means of communication itself – language.

The scholarship which took Heaney away from Mossbawn at the age of eleven to board for six years at the "lonely scarp"[8] of St Columb's College in Derry, not only transported him from a familiar rural environment to an alien urban one, but also replaced a home where there "wasn't much reading done" with a school which gave him a "kind of force-feeding" in "the classic canon of English poetry".[9] The poet's family belonged to a community which was almost as reluctant to speak as it was to read; one where the instinct for reticence characteristic of isolated rural societies was compounded by the peculiar political and social circumstances of Northern Ireland.

If, as Heaney himself recalls in *The Ministry of Fear*,[10] the mere mention of a name like "Seamus" was enough to arouse the suspicion of the Protestant police, far safer for a Catholic to keep his mouth firmly closed. "My people were not like that at all", Heaney has observed, contradicting the popular image of the "typical" Irishman's "great flow of eloquence and wit".[11] On the contrary, the "Mother Ireland" of his childhood was an "old girl" skilled in "elaborate strategies for evasion and compliance", one who shared his own mother's maxim: "Whatever you say, say nothing".[12] In such a tight-lipped rural world, where a father would tease his son for opening a book[13] and where English "poetry" was regarded, if at all, as some remote manifestation of a colonising power, what could be said to a boy who decided to break the ancient farming tradition and make that "poertry"[14] his life?

The need for a sense of place

Heaney himself felt this sense of separation from his family deeply, not only for personal reasons, but also because it threatened his poetic gift. Writing about his poem *The Diviner*, he offers a definition of that gift which helps to locate the source of his problem:

> The diviner resembles the poet in his function of making contact with what lies hidden, and in his ability to make palpable what was sensed or raised.[15]

Heaney believes that poet and diviner both owe their skill to a uniquely intimate and profoundly intuitive sense of place. As the diviner feels for the "pluck of water", so the poet "listens" for his poems. When those poems come, they seem to rise out of the earth like some strange gift from the natural world awarded to the poet for his patient homage:

> they come sometimes like bodies come out of a bog, almost complete, seeming to have been laid down a long time ago, surfacing with a touch of mystery.[16]

Heaney believes in the idea that poetry and place are inextricably linked in this way. When a poet is cut off from his roots and can no longer "listen"[17] to the landscape, he is cut off from the source of his inspiration. This theme emerges again and again throughout Heaney's essays on poetry – for example, in his fascination with Shakespeare's suggestion that "Our poesy is as a gum which oozes/From whence 'tis nourished";[18] or in his praise of Wordsworth as "the first man to articulate the nurture that becomes available to the feelings through dwelling in one dear perpetual place." Like Carson McCullers, he feels that "to know who you are, you have to have a place to come from."[19] As if to clinch the argument, Heaney finds this crucial connection between poem and place enshrined in the very concept of poetry. Tracing the etymology of the word "verse", he discovers that it:

> comes from the Latin *versus* which could mean a line of poetry but could also mean the turn that a ploughman made at the head of the field as he finished one furrow and faced back into another.[20]

Poetry as a weapon

Heaney's need for a sense of place to sustain his poetic talent traps him in a vicious circle. By choosing poetry instead of farming, he distances himself from his family. By distancing himself from his family, he loses touch with the source of his poetic inspiration. The act of creation becomes an act of destruction. It is perhaps in recognition of this paradox that Heaney opens his first collection of verse with an image which transforms the writer's pen from a tool of communication into something that is used when communication breaks down – a weapon:

> Between my finger and my thumb
> The squat pen rests; snug as a gun.

This simile, so jarringly unnatural in itself, so at odds with the values of Mossbawn, and yet strategically placed at the start of the collection, at once introduces a note of alienation into the poems. Two of the uses to which Heaney has put his "weapon" – the laying of ghosts from his past and the recording of the "death" of the "naturalist" in him – have already been discussed; but a gun can also be used to break out from an impossible situation, or to clear a breathing-space. In order to "see himself" as an individual, the poet needs to be able to stand back from the people who are closest to him so that he can place his crucially formative relationships with them in some kind of perspective.

The poet as observer

To achieve this sense of distance, Heaney assumes a stance of remoteness and tight control in the poems about his family. In *Follower* and *Mid-Term Break* particularly, the carefully measured line-lengths, and the formal verse patterns of quatrain and triplet, create a framework of disciplined restraint which is entirely appropriate to the son's coldly unemotional account of his father's loss of strength or the eerily calm manner in which the boy records the death of his brother. In the poems about family, the poet is always seen as an outsider, an observer of other people's actions: following his father's "broad shadow" or looking at him through a window; staring at a dead brother's coffin. Whatever action is taking place on the farm, the poet is excluded from it: while others dig, he sits; while his father ploughs, he trips and falls; when the whole community closes ranks in grief, he is "embarrassed". The closest he comes to joining in the shared activities of the Mossbawn family is merely to offer his working grandfather a bottle of milk, or reluctantly to shake hands with the "old men" who have come to mourn his brother.

Heaney takes his role of observer literally in *Digging*, *Follower* and *Mid-Term Break*, describing only what he sees in terse, factual sentences devoid of comment – the emotionless mask only cracks once, when, in *Mid-Term Break*, he admits to feeling "embarrassed". As elsewhere in his poetry, the effect here is almost entirely visual. Heaney presents the reader with a sequence of selected images and allows them to "speak" for him: a sod of earth rolling over "without breaking" signifies his father's skill with the plough; the picture of a woman coughing out "angry tearless sighs" epitomises his mother's helpless, raging grief. The silence which dominates these three poems enhances this idea of mute witness. Only four words of direct speech are recorded and even these are a ritual expression of sorrow. The only other human sounds to be heard are a woman sighing, a child "yapping", a baby laughing, a man clicking his tongue. Natural noises make up the rest: the "rasping" of a spade; the "squelch and slap/Of soggy peat".

Follower

The pen can also be compared to a gun in the sense that it is used to assert independence and to seek revenge for earlier suffering. In *Follower*, for example, the dramatic structure and image pattern suggest that the relationship portrayed here between father and son should be interpreted in terms of confrontation. The boy is the antithesis of everything his father represents. Against those images of purposeful, pioneering movement which compare the father to a sailing-ship or an explorer, the son is presented as a burden which checks the progress of the older man. The father ploughs with the precision of an expert; but his son is inept. The father works with silent concentration, harnessing the power of the plough-horses with a mere click of his tongue; but the boy breaks that concentration with his futile noise.

Follower is far from being the eulogy it at first seems. The effect created by that dead-pan recital of the father's skills is qualified by the fact that those skills are described in terms of the negative impact they have upon the son. The sight of his father ploughing arouses in the boy a desire for imitation which turns into disappointment – "All I ever did was follow" – and, finally, a sense of inadequacy and rejection: "I was a nuisance". Viewed in this way, the poem represents a release of resentment, an assertion of the child's will against that of the father. To relive the experience in verse is to fight the battle again, this time on the son's conditions, with the weapons that he knows best and his father least – words. The last two lines, so blunt and uncompassionate, deliver a *coup de grace* which completely changes the balance of power in the poem and leaves the son triumphant.

For all that heady sense of power and freedom which the pen/gun analogy gives Heaney, the image is, ultimately, a negative one because it represents a guiltily defiant reaction to the knowledge that he has betrayed his silent farming ancestors. Pursued too far, it would diminish rather than enhance his poetic talent. Every poem which expresses Heaney's alienation from his family removes him further from that sense of place which is the source of his inspiration. If he is to do more as a poet than lay the ghosts of his childhood, poetry and place must be reconciled and the image of the gun replaced by something more positive.

Digging

It is a mark of the sense of conflict and divided loyalty characteristic of **Death of a Naturalist** that Heaney attempts his act of reconciliation in that decisive opening poem, *Digging* – the same work which begins with that contradictory note of alienation. Although the pen/gun analogy sets the tone for so many of the other poems in the collection, here it represents an opening gambit, the departure point for a mental journey which takes the poet, not away from his family, but back towards them.

At the start of that journey, Heaney seems totally cut off from the world of Mossbawn. On a farm dedicated to outdoor manual work, he sits, inside, poised perhaps on the brink of writing something destructive. It is the sight of his father digging which draws him back from this negative act by leading his thoughts away from the confines of the room and out into the wider farming world beyond. The "clean rasping sound" of the spade releases the poet's imagination and sends it travelling back down through succeeding layers of memory where it renews contact first with father, then grandfather, and finally that lost, childhood sense of delight in the natural world.

Reconciliation

When, in the last three lines of the poem, Heaney returns to his starting-point, he comes back with a changed perception of the pen born of a new certainty of purpose. What he has discovered again – this time in creative terms – is that earlier "thrill" of "trusting" his "own background" which he first felt when reading another poet of place, Ted Hughes: the realisation that, as he puts it, "the matter of contemporary poetry was the material of my own life."[21] Rather than allow the pen to separate him from the source of his inspiration, Heaney resolves, in that tersely decisive final line, to use it in a way which will bind him closer to his roots. By saying that he will "dig" with his pen, he places himself beside his father and grandfather. Just as they sustain the life of Mossbawn by digging for turf or planting potatoes, so he, viewing poetry as a "restoration of the culture to itself", will dig down into the community and immortalise what he finds there in the "plants" of his poems.[22]

Where the gun alienates, the spade nurtures. Running counter to the negative impulses of **Death of a Naturalist** comes this positive, creative urge to "enshrine the spirit of the past", as Heaney writes quoting Wordsworth, "For future restoration."[23] The poet will bring poetry and place into creative union and keep faith with his people by reclaiming the "darkness" described in *Personal Helicon*. He will recreate the world of Mossbawn upon the printed page where, transformed through the magic of verse into a "prospect of the mind",[24] it will achieve an immortality that generations of turf-cutters could not win for it.

The poetic landscape of 'Death of a Naturalist'

In order to recreate the world he knew as a child, Heaney must try to experience it again as a small child does – through the senses. For this reason, the poems in **Death of a Naturalist** are filled with colour, tightly packed with images of sight, smell, taste and touch. A well is "Fructified like any aquarium"; the farmhouse "would stink long after churning day"; the "flesh" of blackberries tastes "sweet/Like thickened wine". Throughout the poems, too, the child's voice can be heard, complaining that "It wasn't fair" when the blackberries rot, or explaining how "the mammy frog/Laid hundreds of little eggs and this was/Frogspawn." The emotional experiences described in the poems are conveyed in children's terms. In *Death of a Naturalist,* the boy's changed perception of the frogs is expressed in his fear "That if I dipped my hand the spawn would clutch it"; while in *Mid-Term Break* the son's embarrassment at having to act as public representative of the family contrasts powerfully with his parents more conventionally adult response to grief.

Death of a Naturalist presents a precisely realised picture of the world of Mossbawn, its people, their work, their customs and their language. The sense of place is intense: from the creative centre where the poet sits writing at his window in *Digging*, the eye looks down on the flowerbeds of the farm garden, moves out past the barn and the byre, past "hayfields, cornfields and potato-drills" in *Blackberry-Picking* to the school, the flax-dam, Toner's bog. The people of Mossbawn move in and out of the poems, usually too absorbed in their work to speak: the poet's father ploughs, his mother takes "first turn" on churning day; Miss Walls gives her rudimentary biology lesson, "Big Jim Evans" offers consolation for the death of a brother.

The work these people do and their places of work are minutely observed, sometimes in a whole poem such as *The Barn* or *Churning Day*. Always, the poet's eye seeks out the telling signs of expertise – his father's "course boot nestled on the lug" of his spade, his grandfather "Nicking and slicing neatly" at the turf. Every aspect of working life at Mossbawn is lovingly recorded by Heaney, as though he is anxious lest any part of the memory escape: the working implements (spade, pitchfork, plough, harness, "two-lugged sacks"), the seasonal rituals (frog-spawn collecting in spring, blackberrying in late August). Even seemingly insignificant details are noticed: the way milk is "Corked sloppily with paper" or tea is served in "bright canfuls".

Language and diction

Heaney's love of Mossbawn is also revealed through the language he uses to describe it. Far from being self-conscious about the specialised farming vocabulary of his home or feeling obliged to modify it for the benefit of his audience, he shows off the familiar words of childhood – "townland", "headrig" or "whisky muddler" – as proudly as a dialect poet might. But more than this, one of the most outstanding features of **Death of a Naturalist** is the impression the collection gives of a poet who, having just discovered the joy and the power of sound, is determined to exploit every linguistic trick of alliteration, assonance or onomatopoeia and explore every register from soprano to bass, in order that he might recapture all the noises and silences of his home.

The sheer range of sounds created by Heaney is remarkable. Take, for example, a phrase from *Digging*: "the spade sinks into gravelly ground". Here, the "clean rasping" noise made when the father's spade hits gravel is precisely evoked by the crisp alliteration of the letters "s" and "g". The open "a" and "ou" sounds in the phrase suggest the depth and the yielding nature of the ground, and contrast powerfully with the sharp closed "i" and hard "k" of "sink" as the spade bites into the earth. The four stresses on "spade", "sinks", "gravelly" and "ground" create a heavy, falling rhythm which, coming to rest on that final, definite "d", mimics perfectly the downward strokes of the digger.

At the other end of the tonal range lies the description of the "angry frogs" in *Death of a Naturalist*: "their loose necks pulsed like sails". In this phrase, sibilance, assonance and the open vowel sounds create a sinister whispering effect, emphasised by a regular stress pattern which imitates the repulsive breathing of the "slime kings", and by the masterly way in which the long, soft "uls" sound of "pulsed" smothers the plosive "p" which precedes it, like a muffled explosion.

Always, Heaney searches for the combination of sounds which will catch precisely the action described. When he observes, in *Blackberry-Picking*, how the "big dark blobs burned", each hard monosyllable falls into the line as solidly as a berry into the collecting can. In *Churning Day*, the quick, light interplay of the alliterated "s" with the letters "p" and "t" recreates beautifully the action of butter-making in the phrase: "the pat and slap of small spades on wet lumps". Even when Heaney is trying to describe something unpleasant, it is the same exuberant love of sound which dominates the line, as in the bitterly plosive "pits turned pus into filthy mounds" from *At a Potato Digging*.

Summary and conclusion

This joyful music-making, so different from that other, terse voice of alienation, epitomises, finally, the contradiction which lies at the heart of Heaney's first book of verse. Death, both literal and metaphorical, is the theme which binds these disparate poems together; and death is something which inspires powerful, ambivalent emotions in those left behind: on the one hand, a sense of release and new-found independence; on the other, a sense of guilt and a desire to recapture what has been lost. **Death of a Naturalist** is torn by these conflicting impulses: the desire to escape from a lost world is matched by the desire to return to it; poetry as obligation is countered by poetry as joyful self-assertion; poem is ranged against place. "Poetry is out of the quarrel with ourselves",[25] Heaney writes. By articulating that quarrel, and by trying to resolve it, he found his poetic voice.

Notes and References

Unless otherwise stated, all the quotations are from Seamus Heaney's own essays.

1. William Wordsworth, *Intimations of Immortality from Recollections of Early Childhood.*
2. *A Poet's Childhood*, **The Listener**, 11 November 1971, p. 660.
3. *Mossbawn*, **Preoccupations: Selected Prose 1968–1978**. London and Boston, Mass.: Faber, 1980, p. 19.
4. Ibid., p. 17. The experience is examined in greater detail in the poem *Cauled* from a collection by Heaney called **Stations**, Belfast, Ulsterman Publications, 1975.
5. *Canticles to the Earth*, **Preoccupations**, p. 192.
6. *A Poet's Childhood*, **The Listener**, p. 661.
7. *Feeling into Words*, **Preoccupations**, p. 41.
8. Heaney, *The Ministry of Fear*, **North**, London: Faber, 1975.
9. *Mossbawn*, **Preoccupations**, p. 21, p. 26.
10. **North**, p. 64.
11. Heaney, interview, in Monie Begley, **Rambles in Ireland**: Old Greenwich, Conn.: Devin-Adair, 1977, p. 164.
12. *Celtic Fringe, Viking Fringe*, **The Listener**, 21 August 1969, p. 255.
13. *Mossbawn*, **Preoccupations**, p. 21.
14. Ibid., p. 26.
15. *Feeling into Words*, **Preoccupations**, p.. 48.
16. *Belfast*, **Preoccupations**, p. 34.
17. *The Makings of a Music*, **Preoccupations**, p. 63.
18. *The Fire i' the Flint*, **Preoccupations**, p. 79.
19. *The Sense of Place*, **Preoccupations**, p. 145, p. 135.
20. *The Makings of a Music*, **Preoccupations**, p. 65.
21. James Randall, *An Interview with Seamus Heaney*, **Ploughshares**, 5,3, 1979, p. 14.
22. *Feeling into Words*, **Preoccupations**, p. 41.
23. Ibid. The quote is from Wordsworth's poem *The Prelude*.
24. *Mossbawn*, **Preoccupations**, p. 20.
25. *Belfast*, **Preoccupations**, p. 34.

Chapter Two

'Door into the Dark'

A new sense of confidence

To break fresh ground, a poet must feel that he has achieved a coming to terms with the pressures of his past, and a sense of confidence in his ability to take risks and meet new creative challenges. By 1969, the year in which Heaney's second collection of verse was published, he felt secure on both counts. The title of that second book, **Door into the Dark**, has a defiant, bracing ring to it, and suggests a picture of a man who has voluntarily turned his back on the familiar in order to set out on an exciting voyage of discovery.

Heaney had worked through the problems inherent in his childhood relationship with his family by writing about them in **Death of a Naturalist**. By 1969, the claims for independence made in his first book had been effectively realised: as an established lecturer in English at Queen's University, Belfast, Heaney could feel that he was no longer stumbling in his father's "hob-nailed wake" but working successfully on his own terms. Perhaps more significantly, marriage and the birth of his first child meant his position within the family had altered from son or "follower" to husband and father in his own right. It is a measure of the peace which Heaney now felt he had achieved in his relationship with his parents that **Door into the Dark** is dedicated to them.

By 1969, Heaney had good reason to feel that, as he put it, "I could do this poetry thing too".[1] Not only was he making a living from teaching the subject, but he had also known the pleasure of seeing his faith in his poetic voice triumphantly vindicated by critical acclaim. Hailed by one reviewer as "the best first book of poems I've read for some time",[2] **Death of a Naturalist** went through three impressions in the year of its publication.

Poetic influences

The sense of confidence generated by critical success was reinforced by Heaney's discovery that he was not the only young Ulsterman engaged in the eccentric business of writing verse. Credit for this was due to the critic and lecturer Philip Hobsbaum who, when he came to teach at Queen's in 1960, kept "open house for poetry", turning his flat in Fitzwilliam Street into a centre where, on Monday nights, local writers could meet to read and discuss their work. It was here that Heaney befriended other young Ulster poets such as Michael Longley and Derek Mahon, and here too that, as he recalls, Hobsbaum moved "disparate elements into a single action", so that writers who had felt themselves "islanded about the place" could now come together with the shared identity and common purpose of a literary "Group".[3]

Older Irish poets, too, offered Heaney reassurance by showing him that others had experienced the creative tensions described in **Death of a Naturalist**. The work of Patrick Kavanagh, whose **Collected Poems** appeared in the year *Digging* was written, 1964, became a source of particular strength. Kavanagh's move from the family farm at Inniskeen to Dublin in pursuit of poetry recalls Heaney's own journey from Mossbawn to Belfast. Moreover, his evocation of "the world of childhood and the attendant sense of loss"[4] within the context of the "buried life" of rural Ireland, seemed to validate the younger writer's own poetic themes; while his declaration that "I have lived in important places"[5] asserts the right of "parochial"[6] poetry such as Heaney's to appear before the widest audience.

Imagery of movement

Encouraged by personal success and the support or example of other Irish poets, Heaney's own creative temperament urged him to make his second book an act of fresh exploration. Like Kavanagh again, he had no desire to imitate what he describes as the "parnassian" mode of poetry-writing in which "technical discoveries originally made while delivering a poem of the first intensity" are deployed "a second time".[7] For Heaney, creative satisfaction comes from "extension"; no sooner is he "confirmed by the visitation of the last poem" then he feels "threatened by the elusiveness of the next one".[8] Artistic vitality is sustained by moving forward – to stay still, to hesitate before the door into the dark, is to stagnate.

Heaney's second volume is in fact informed by a sense of movement. Sometimes it has a purposeful, epic quality, as when in *Beyond Sargasso* the eel, a "muscled icicle", battles its way across the Atlantic, or when the "Croppies" tackle the Protestant yeomanry "on the hike". Elsewhere, it is movement for the sheer joy of movement's sake: in *The Peninsula* and *Night Drive*, for example, this sense of release is invoked by the idea of just getting into a car and driving.

The spirit of purposeful or spontaneous and exhilerating movement characteristic of **Door into the Dark** is given tangible expression by the image-pattern of flowing water which emerges in the poems. In **Death of a Naturalist**, that water "festered" in stagnant flax-dams, lay trapped in wells, or had to be carefully tracked to its "secret stations" by an expert; but here it flows freely across the landscape through trenches, drains, sunk-pipes, sluice gates and streams. No longer controlled or hunted by man, water is now the master, claiming a "victim every year" from the fishermen whose lives it dominates, or even shaping the destiny of Ireland by carrying succeeding waves of invaders to its shores.

It is this image-pattern of free-flowing, irresistible water which marks **Door into the Dark** as a work of creative release; for Heaney describes the act of poetic creation in precisely the same terms. Since the poet is like a water-diviner, his moment of inspiration comes when the "secret stations" of "Spring water" break free as though from a collapsing dam. The "best moments", Heaney observes in the essay *Feeling into Words*, "are those when your mind seems to implode and words and images rush of their own accord into the vortex". *Les vers donnes*, the "given line", releases the poet's imagination so that it flows from one image to another in a quickening current, while he simply "surrenders" to these "energies that spring within the centre of the mind".[9]

Undine

The process is clearly described in Heaney's account of *Undine*. From the "dark pool of the sound of the word" pours a cumulatively powerful, underground stream of images: the word "unda", a wave, flows into "undine", a "water-sprite", which in turn uncovers a childhood memory of watching "a man clearing out an old spongy growth from a drain", before surfacing at last in a "more conscious reading of the myth as being about the liberating, humanizing effect of sexual encounter".[10]

If the image of running water is a metaphor for the act of composition, then *Undine* also serves to locate the source of that creative stream which runs so freely through **Door into the Dark**. This poem provides the key to an understanding of Heaney's second volume of verse, for in it he reappraises the declaration of artistic intent made in that earlier and equally important work, *Digging*. The two poems have several similarities. The dramatic structure of both is based on a movement from sterile confinement to triumphant release. In *Undine* the spirit which is imprisoned in its "own drains" by "grey silt" at the start of the poem disperses itself, at the end, "for love". Again as in *Digging*, the act of liberation is achieved – through literally here – by a man with a spade. However, *Undine* does not simply represent a rewriting of Heaney's earlier statement. It is in the subtle variations between this poem and its model that the poetic concerns of **Door into the Dark** emerge.

The most significant difference lies in the identity and relationship of the characters portrayed in *Undine*. The two protagonists of *Digging* were a particular father and his son, living on a particular Irish farm; but here the digger, stripped of personality and described only as "he", becomes a timeless, universal symbol of the labourer. The narrator of the poem has changed even more dramatically: the earth-bound farmer's son is replaced by something magically elusive, at once a stream of water, or a mythological creature, or an image of poetic inspiration. Freed from temporal ties, the relationship between the digger and this protean spirit suffers from none of those ambiguous feelings which keep son apart from father in *Digging*. On the contrary, they embrace each other with sexual passion, and the words which describe their meeting are those a woman might use about her lover: "I ran quick for him"; "He explored me ... completely"; "I swallowed his trench/Gratefully, dispersing myself for love".

In *Undine* as in *Digging*, Heaney revives that potent image of the labourer and his spade to pay tribute once again to the fact that the rural working world is the source of his poetic inspiration; and once again, in the declaration that "I alone/Could give him subtle increase and reflection", the poet declares his solidarity with this world and dedicates his art to its preservation and celebration. Now, however, because Heaney no longer feels threatened by Mossbawn, he can devote the whole of his artistic talent to the task instead of speaking in the ambiguous tones of **Death of a Naturalist**. For this reason, his new declaration of intent has a boastful sound to it; the aggressively abrupt, uncertain claiming of kin which ended *Digging* is replaced by a proud and secure "I alone". As "professionally/Unfussed" as the water-diviner, the poet feels that he possesses a unique gift. Heaney no longer needs to disguise his pen in order to gain acceptance within the community, for through his role as spokesman he has won fame and prestige for it and an honoured place for himself.

Secure in his position, Heaney feels confident enough to extend his role. In **Death of a Naturalist**, he had to "dig" into the soil of Mossbawn in order to gain self-knowledge; now he intends to go deeper still, to place Mossbawn itself in perspective by exploring the rural Irish society which created it. The digger in *Undine* is portrayed as a timeless, universal figure because he represents, not one particular working man, but all those Irish people who have learned through bitter experience that "life in the secluded spot is no book of pastoral hours but an enervating round of labour and lethargy".[11.]

Experiments with metrical forms

This extension of theme is reflected in a corresponding willingness to experiment with metrical forms. In several of these poems, the heavy, decasyllabic verses of **Death of a Naturalist** give way to shorter, rhythmically more adventurous lines, of two and three stresses each, which offer a visual representation of the poet's theme. The terse, spare, concentrated quatrains of works like *Bogland* or *The Plantation* descend like shafts sunk into the earth, forcing the reader to proceed downwards slowly and thoughtfully from line to line so that he might follow as nearly as possible the poet's own experience of this deeper "digging".

Beyond Sargasso

Most technically ambitious of all these "shape-poems" is *Beyond Sargasso* where – counterpointed in a masterly fashion against a rigid structure of six syllables to the line – sound, rhythm and line-length create an aural and visual pattern of expansion and contraction that evokes precisely the eel's outward and home-bound journeys through the ebb and flow of the Atlantic currents.

As the eel grows and swims away to sea, so the lean, dental consonants of the opening expand into lines rich with sibilance, alliteration and open vowel sounds which combine, in turn, with the lazy, sliding motion of the stressed syllables in "drifted" and "insinuating" to create a sense of quickening life and increasingly powerful movement. The second, "incoming" paragraph of the poem reverses the pattern of the "outgoing" first from crescendo to diminuendo. The smooth-flowing line of the eel's wide-ranging "orbit" breaks, literally, upon the pivotal word "Against" and the hard, punctuated monosyllables which follow it, so that the second paragraph seems to offer an almost physical barrier to the homeward journey. Once the barrier is breached, the broken line is restored and flows triumphantly again into alliteration and long vowel, until with a deft flick of the body on those final dental consonants, the eel disappears into the sand and the cycle begins again.

The widening poetic landscape

The geographical range of *Beyond Sargasso* typifies a general broadening of the poetic landscape in **Door into the Dark**. Since Heaney now feels capable of speaking for a whole people rather than just one community, the poems of his second volume reach out, beneath a sky "tall as over a runway", across the entire country from Lough Neagh to Wicklow and on to "the most westerly Blasket". Political boundaries are ignored. Heaney's feeling that his territory now included the whole of Ireland, rather than just Mossbawn, was enhanced by the fact that the beginning of his poetic career coincided with the development in Ulster of a new concern for Irish culture. General movements like the revival of interest in traditional music, and specific events such as the opening of the Ulster Folk Museum in 1964, or the Belfast Festival in the following year, all offered a national sanction to the poet's "archaeology of the imagination".[12]

One work from this period which particularly helped to convince Heaney that the world of rural Ireland was academically "respectable" and something to be valued, was a book which appeared in 1957 called **Irish Folk Ways**, written by the Director of the Institute of Irish Studies at Queen's, E. Estyn Evans. In Evans' declaration that "knowledge of ways of life that have altered little for centuries is passing away",[13] Heaney could hear an echo of his own preoccupation with loss; and part of his intention in **Door into the Dark** is to offer a poetic response to the Professor's warning.

The same observational skills which recorded the daily working routine of Mossbawn are redeployed here in a wider survey of vanishing traditional crafts. Heaney's concern is to be totally faithful to the people for whom he is speaking, to show exactly how a thatcher "snipped at straw and sharpened ends of rods", or a fisherman collected worms for eel-bait "in the field at midnight". Once more, his photographer's eye seeks out the quintessential detail which brings the whole experience to life: the "hiss" made when a new horseshoe "toughens in water", in *The Forge* or the feel of seed in the hand described in *The Wife's Tale*, "hard as shot,/Innumerable and cool." Again Heaney's affection for his subject is revealed through the joyful sounds he uses to describe it: in the alliteration and rich, open vowels of "wakes are enwound as the catch/On the morning water", for example, or the brittle staccato of "the hammered anvil's short-pitched ring".

The magical world-view

The lives of blacksmith, thatcher, fisherman, traditional musician and farmer's wife are recorded and preserved here as in a documentary film; but it is a measure of Heaney's confidence in his vision and in his sense of identity that he is not content merely to play the passive role of social historian in these poems. Instead, he actively asserts the values that these people represent as a viable alternative to twentieth-century materialism. In *The Forge*, for example, the blacksmith's hard-won skill and individual craftsmanship are ranged against that belief in anonymous mass-production which has replaced the "clatter/Of hoofs" with "traffic ... flashing in rows". Just as the poet approves of the smith's decision to turn his back on that traffic and "beat real iron out", so again, in *Up the Shore*, he applauds as "fair play" the fishermen's determination to "confront" the eels "one by one" rather than use "new gates and tanks" to "lift five hundred stone in one go".

Heaney's stance here is no affectation: he is not only proud of these people but actually invests their work with a magical or religious significance. The smith's anvil is seen as something fabulous and yet at the same time as representative of permanent values – "Horned as a unicorn" but also "Set there immoveable". More than this, it is "an altar" at which the smith, a priest in the religion of craftsmanship and an artist as well, "expends himself in shape and music." Similarly, the thatcher is seen as a magician who changes straw into gold and leaves ordinary mortals "gaping at his Midas touch"; the fiddler in *The Given Note* charms music "out of the night"; and the woman in *The Wife's Tale* passes among the field-workers like a physical embodiment of the undine, leaving them "Spread out, unbuttoned, grateful, under the trees".

The almost reverential tone of voice with which Heaney describes this threatened peasant world marks a development in his conception of the poet's relationship to society. Far from simply celebrating and recording the working lives of his people, he invests the poems of **Door into the Dark** with a moral function, using them to identify, consolidate and display the virtues of the society he serves, so that its members might receive from him as from Kavanagh, "an image of themselves that nourished their sense of themselves",[14] and thus learn to defend their cultural heritage against the external economic pressures which threaten its existence. *A Lough Neagh Sequence* was written, not for "the ear",[15] but "for the fishermen". By introducing this note of moral purpose into his poetry, Heaney moves closer to assuming the mantle of a national or, more precisely, a tribal poet. He makes further claim to the title when, writing again with the tribal poet's intention of bringing a sense of self-knowledge and self-esteem to his people, he lays before them certain critical moments in their history.

The theme of history

This particular door into the dark, already partially opened in poems like *At a Potato Digging* from **Death of a Naturalist**, is explored further in *Requiem for the Croppies*. Faced now with a theme broader and more public than anything he had ever attempted before, Heaney launches himself into the dangerous waters of Irish history – guided by his belief in poetry as "a restoration of the culture to itself."[16] In order to restore their culture to his people, he must select those episodes from the history of Ireland which fundamentally affected them. As he did when recording life at Mossbawn or the work of craftsmen, he must commemorate what happened and explain what it was like to be there.

This didactic tone emerges in both *At a Potato Digging* and *Requiem for the Croppies*, as Heaney tells how "wild higgledy skeletons/ scoured the land in "'forty-five", or how the rebellion of 1798 ended with a "fatal conclave" on "Vinegar Hill". As before, Heaney's didacticism here is not that of an orthodox researcher; instead, he selects from the story those details which would make most sense to a peasant community and have most impact on them. The horror of the 1845 famine is epitomised in an image which would strike a chord in any farmer who had known what it was like to see a vital crop fail:

> The new potato, sound as stone,
> putrefied when it had lain
> three days in the long clay pit.

In *Requiem for the Croppies*, the potential for revolutionary change which the rebellion brought is evoked in a line which completely overturns the established social hierarchy of an Irish village: "The priest lay behind ditches with the tramp."

Writing for a people who are "not literary",[17] Heaney uses the techniques of folk poetry to tell his story. The heavy rhythm and inevitable rhyme scheme of *Requiem for the Croppies* give the poem the ritualistic character of a lament, while Part III of *At a Potato Digging* has the quatrain and rhyming couplet structure of a simple ballad. Indeed, so anxious is Heaney to achieve the effect of folk naivety here that the poem sometimes topples into banality, as when the humble word "it" is forced to take the weight of a final rhyme at the end of the second verse. Like the ballad-maker, Heaney tells his human story in terms of the natural world: "Hope" rots "like a marrow"; "beaks of famine" attack the starving who are "grubbing, like plants, in the bitch earth"; the hillside "blushed" at the massacre of the "Croppies". That sense of the macabre or supernatural which is such a prevalent feature of the ballad world can also be found here, too, where "blind-eyed" skeletons "scoured the land in "'forty-five", or one of the "Croppies" comes back from the dead to tell how "They buried us without shroud or coffin".

The connection between landscape and history

Heaney's aim here is not simply to record his people's history in terms they will understand. Beyond this, the two poems represent the beginning of an "attempt to define and interpret the present by bringing it into significant relationship with the past".[18] The poet will use history as a means of teaching the tribe how to survive in the future. The historical message which emerges from *At a Potato Digging* and *Requiem for the Croppies* is that "the experience of life on the land" is "perhaps the most formative" experience "the majority of Irish people" have ever known and that "the land itself" provides "the stable element" in "the history of Ireland".[19]

Events which took place on the land in the past have profoundly influenced modern Irish society. When that land became the "bitch earth" in 1845, the Irish peasantry were "grafted with a great sorrow" which hurt so deeply that, even today, "you still smell the running sore". When the "Croppies" rebelled in 1798, it was their knowledge of the land which enabled them to move "quick and sudden" in their "own country" and thus resist a technologically superior enemy. In defeat the land provided the memorial their enemies had tried to deny them – a potent, living memorial which not only flowered literally, but also grew metaphorically through the years, flourishing at last in triumphant revenge as the "'right rose tree' of 1916".[20]

The connection between national history and the landscape explored in *At a Potato Digging* and *Requiem for the Croppies* is a major concern of Heaney's second volume. The poems reveal a growing awareness of Ireland as a place where the "present is suffused with the past" – a country haunted by the ghosts of the peoples who shaped it. "Someone had always been there", Heaney oberves in

The Plantation, "Though always you were alone"; and in *Shoreline* he can hear "the Danes" or "the chinking Normans" coming back on the waves to reclaim the lands they once held. Place names acquire a new significance, becoming for him as for another Ulster poet, John Montague, "sounding lines, rods to plumb the depths of a shared and diminished culture":[21] "Strangford, Arklow, Carrickfergus,/Belmullet and Ventry" stand like "forgotten ... sentries", posted by armies that have vanished for ever.

Bogland as a poetic metaphor

It was by returning to the boglands of Mossbawn that Heaney found an image which might make a connection between "memory" and "national consciousness"[22] and also give poetic expression to his sense of the relationship between a country's landscape and its past. Ever since the days when, as he recalls in the essay **Mossbawn**, he had first shunned "the moss" as "forbidden ground" and then "betrothed" himself to it by bathing naked in a "moss-hole",[23] the bog had represented for Heaney a repository of powerful memories "with associations reaching back into early childhood." At the same time he recognised the boglands as being, literally, a storage-place; for as a boy he had been brought up on stories of how butter might be "kept fresh for a great number of years under the peat", or, more dramatically, of how "the skeleton of an elk had been taken out of a bog nearby". As Heaney grew older, he came to realise that the history of his country lay buried beneath his own homelands:

> I began to get an idea of bog as the memory of the landscape, or as a landscape that remembered everything that happened in and to it. In fact, if you go round the National Museum in Dublin, you will realize that a great proportion of the most cherished material heritage of Ireland was "found in a bog".[24]

Bogland

Although the poem which draws all these ideas together is placed last in **Door into the Dark**, *Bogland*, like *Undine* provides a key to the whole collection; for here Heaney describes the final and most mysterious stage of his voyage of discovery. The poem was written in response to the idea of "the frontier and the west as an important myth in the American consciousness". By linking his quest to the almost legendary journeys made by those settlers who pioneered a trail across the New World, the poet brings the image-pattern of movement which has dominated his second volume to an epic conclusion – for it is an epic theme that concerns him here.

The search for an Irish myth

"Our pioneers", Heaney declares in response to the American experience, "keep striking/Inwards and downwards"; and the purpose of his final journey in **Door into the Dark** is to follow those "pioneers" by digging for something much deeper than the relics of recorded, Christian, Irish history. To complete his duties as tribal poet, he means to trace his people's most important and enduring relationship – their relationship with the land – back to its ancient, pre-Christian source. On behalf of his mythically powerful craftsmen and fishermen, and in defiance of the American vision which has done so much in the twentieth century to threaten their world, Heaney establishes and explores "the bog as an answering Irish myth."[25]

An essay called *The God in the Tree* helps to clarify this aim. Here, describing the creative tensions apparent in the works of the early Irish nature poets who wrote in the centuries following the conversion of Ireland by St. Patrick, Heaney has observed that their "imagination" takes its "colouring" from "two very different elements":

> On the one hand, there is the *pagus*, the pagan wilderness, green, full-throated, unrestrained; on the other hand there is the lined book, the Christian *disciplina*, the sense of a spiritual principle and a religious calling that transcends the almost carnal lushness of nature itself.

To follow the relationship between the land and his people to its deepest roots in the subconscious folk-memory, Heaney had to do something bolder than these first exponents of the art would have dared: to reach back beyond the constraints of Christian *disciplina* to that earlier world of the *pagus*: "a world older and darker and greener than the world of early Christian Ireland". Renouncing St. Patrick in favour of his ancient, pagan enemy Oisin, symbol of "unregenerate natural man", Heaney reinterprets his own nature poetry by tracing a connection between "the role of the *file*, the official poet in historic times," and "the role of the druid in archaic times." The idea of poet as druid excites his imagination, he writes, because:

> the root of the word "druid" is related to *doire*, the oak grove, and through that the poet is connected with the mysteries of the grove, and the poetic imagination is linked with the barbaric life of the wood, with Oisin rather than with Patrick.[26]

What sets Heaney apart from other nature poets writing in English today is the fact that, in order to fulfil his obligations as tribal poet, he is prepared to take this druidic role upon himself and look at his native landscape through the eyes of Oisin.

Landscape interpreted as myth

Viewed in this way, Ireland becomes a place which is "sacramental, instinct with signs, implying a system of reality beyond the visible realities" – beyond "buttercups and ladysmock", "primroses and ... celandines", the "single thorn-tree,"[27] lies an invisible world populated by "deities"[28] of "the old religion"[29] who are "shrouded in the living matrices of stones and trees, immanent in the natural world".[30]

These spirits haunt the landscape of **Door into the Dark**, transforming it into an active, living force which pulls men towards it mysteriously and irresistibly. Even on foreign soil, as in *Night Drive* for example, the names of the French towns draw the poet on "relentlessly" through the darkness; but back home in Ireland, on native ground, his vulnerability to the power of these "deities" of place is much greater. The word "vulnerability" is used advisedly here, because the spirits "immanent in the natural world" have nothing to do with the Christian vision of love and compassion. On the contrary, Heaney portrays them as dark, predatory forces. In *The Peninsula*, for example, they seem to close in upon the driver at dusk as "horizons drink down sea and hill," or "The ploughed field swallows the whitewashed gable". Elsewhere, their power is described in more sinister terms, as though the landscape was trying to entice the unwary to itself in order to trap them. Thus in *Bogland*, the "eye" is "wooed into the cyclop's eye/Of a tarn"; and those who are drawn beyond the safety of "the picnickers' belt" in *The Plantation* by the sinister "hush and ... mush/Of its whispering treadmill", feel so threatened by the ancient woodland that they turn back anxiously to the reassuring twentieth-century "hum of the traffic".

The poet as High Priest

These modern-day interlopers who flee in confused alarm from the plantation are contrasted in the poem with the narrator who, though susceptible to the power of the wood's mystery, is permitted to walk through its "charmed rings". Like all gods, those of the Irish countryside have their own favoured priests to whom they grant revelation and through whom they speak to the people. As explorer and interpreter of the landscape, the druid/poet Heaney is one such figure: the poems of **Door into the Dark** flow as confidently and easily from him as running water, for he is inspired by the spirits of Ireland. If he describes the craftsmen of rural Ulster in terms of reverential awe it is because he regards them as co-religionists. Like him, they achieve a special intimacy with the gods of place by entering into a trance-like communion with them, either through the celebration of the mysteries of true craftsmanship like the smith who beats "real iron out" upon the "altar" of his anvil, or by seeking revelation in a lonely place like the musician in *The Given Note*.

History as sacrifice

Pen, hammer and fiddle are elevated as the badges of a religious elite; but from the rest of the working people of rural Ireland the dark gods of the landscape demand homage and sacrifice. Heaney first explores this idea in *At a Potato Digging* where the stooping and bending of the labourers is described in terms of an ancient religious ritual:

>   Centuries
> Of fear and homage to the famine god
> Toughen the muscles behind their humbled knees,
> Make a seasonal altar of the sod.

Behind the "visible realities" of "turf" and "drill" lies the deity of the soil, the "black/Mother" – a capricious fertility goddess who might grant the favour of a potato harvest in return for the sacrifice of exhausting physical labour, but is just as likely to manifest herself as the "bitch earth" and destroy "Millions". Looked at through the eyes of Oisin, the Great Famine of 1845 is seen not as a comprehensible event which can be rationally analysed by economist and historian, but as the retribution of an illogical and vengeful god. In **Door into the Dark**, the 1798 rebellion is interpreted in the same terms of folk-legend. Taking the nickname of the rebels literally, Heaney describes their defeat as though it were a fertility myth of sacrificial death and regeneration: cut down in "Terraced thousands" for the sake of Ireland, the sufferings of this human crop are rewarded by a miraculous transformation and rebirth when "in August the barley grew up out of the grave."

This vision of rural life as a ritual of sacrifice and regeneration is not simply perceived at moments of crisis such as 1798 and 1845; it lies at the heart of the working experience. In *A Lough Neagh Sequence*, worm, eel, lake, ocean and fisherman all play their allotted part in the ancient, yearly cycle of pursuit, combat, death and rebirth. For each participant, the process has the inevitability of a ceremony: the worm "needs to come, out of the clay"; the eel must follow the Atlantic current "sure as the satellite's/insinuating pull"; the fishermen have to set to work "'Once the season's in'". Bound together in a common ritual, each creature is linked to the others by a sacrificial chain: worm is linked to eel, eel to fisherman and, most dramatically of all, the fishermen are bound to the lough; for to these men as to the potato-diggers, the spirit of the place is a jealous god who must be placated with nothing less than a human sacrifice: "'The Lough will claim a victim every year.'"

It is with this discovery that the journey of **Door into the Dark** comes to an end. The "answering Irish myth" which controls the relationship between Heaney's people and Ireland is a harsh myth. It explains existence in terms of suffering. Bound to the landscape, man is totally dependent upon its capriciousness or its cruelty for his survival. Life is created and then sacrificed in a timeless ritual of death and regeneration. The history of rural Ireland moves in cycles; its events are at once ancient and yet immediate: the "stooping" of the potato-diggers recurs "mindlessly as autumn"; the ceremony of the eel-hunt began "when the lough first spawned" and yet starts again as though for the first time "'Once the season's in'." Their awareness of the power of the landscape and the cyclical nature of its history makes the people fatalistic: the fishermen of Lough Neagh refuse to learn to swim, even though "one hour floating's sure to land them safely", because they know that the lough exacts an annual toll for its eels.

Reconciliation with nature

This sense of having looked right to the heart of the relationship between land and people brings an unexpected serenity to Heaney's work. The pagan vision of Oisin might reveal a landscape devoid of Christ's compassion, but it also removes from the observer "the weight of Christianity in all its rebuking aspects",[31] so that he no longer has to consider that landscape in terms of his own guilt.

On the rare occasions when the guilt of Heaney's first book does re-emerge in **Door into the Dark**, it achieves no more that a temporary hold over him. Thus in *Vision*, for example, the sight of a "jellied road" of eels moving through the grass like "hatched fears" does not shatter some childishly sentimental view of nature as the "great slime kings" did in *Death of a Naturalist*. On the contrary, this particular picture of "sinewed slime" reaches out from a world that is gone for ever to confirm, momentarily, the "horrid cable" of a youthful fantasy; and it touches, not a small boy from primary school, but an adult capable of rationalising that "mealy rope" of lice into nothing more dangerous than "eels crossing land".

In place of Christian guilt, the druid/poet offers a pantheism that may be cruel but can also, as Heaney observes in *The God in the Tree*, perceive "the world as light", celebrating the unique part played by each living thing in the pattern of creation with a hedonistic "delight in the elemental" and a "surge towards praise". By following the early Irish poets in their espousal of "the god in the tree as a source of poetic inspiration", Heaney learns to "seek out and watch and love Nature, in its tiniest phenomena as in its grandest", and to bless what might once have disturbed him. Thus, in *At Ardboe Point*, he refuses the temptation to place the mosquitoes "under a lens" and distort them into a "visitation" "More drastic than Pharaoh's". To his now "rinsed eyes",[32] that "smoke of flies" is transfigured into "our innocent, shuttling/Choirs". No creature's part in the life-cycle goes unnoticed or unappreciated. In *A Lough Neagh Sequence*, for example, the heroic journey of the eel "through the weltering dark" of the Atlantic is of course commemorated, but so also is the humbler service of the worms – those "Innocent ventilators of the ground" without whom the sacrificial ritual would not be complete.

Summary and conclusion

The title of **Door into the Dark** promises challenge, exploration, a self-confident willingness to take risks; and this second volume of poetry delivers those promises. Trusting in the increasing authority of his voice, Heaney searches now for nothing less ambitious than the role of national poet. He explores his people's fundamentally important relationship with the land to its dark, pagan source, in order to bring them back an "answering Irish myth" with which to counter the threat of twentieth-century materialism. Nothing states the intentions of **Door into the Dark** more clearly than Heaney's comment upon the work of the most famous Irish poet of all:

> Yeats and his friends embarked upon a deliberately counter-cultural movement to reinstate the fairies, to make the world more magical than materialistic, and to elude the social and political interpretations of society in favour of a legendary and literary vision of race.[33]

It is in the footsteps of no less a figure than Yeats that Heaney now wanted to go; and in the very year that **Door into the Dark** was published, events were to take place in Ireland which made the services of a poet of Yeatsian stature – one whose vision could plumb the depths of darkness and yet also perceive "the world as light" – more necessary than ever.

Notes and References

Unless otherwise stated, all the quotations are from **Preoccupations**.

1. *Feeling into Words*, p. 42.
2. C.B. Cox, *The Painter's Eye*, **Spectator**, 20 May 1966, p. 638.
3. *Belfast*, pp. 29, 29, 28, 29.
4. *After the Synge-song*, **The Listener**, 13 January 1972, p. 55.
5. *From Monaghan to the Grand Canal*, pp. 116, 116.
6. *The Sense of Place*, p. 137.
7. *From Monaghan to the Grand Canal*, pp. 116, 116, 117.
8. *Feeling into Words*, p. 54.
9. Ibid., pp. 54, 61, 61, 61, 63.
10. Ibid., p. 53.
11. *From Monaghan to the Grand Canal*, p. 122.
12. *A Poet's Childhood*, **The Listener**, 11 November 1971, p. 661.
13. E. Estyn Evans, **Irish Folk Ways**, London: Routledge, 1957, p. xv. See also Blake Morrison, **Seamus Heaney** London and New York: Methuen, 1982, p. 31.
14. *The Sense of Place*, p. 137.
15. Heaney, *Exposure*, **North**, p. 72, London: Faber, 1975.
16. *The Makings of a Music*, p. 61.
17. Heaney, interview, in John Haffenden, **Viewpoints** London: Faber, 1981, p. 63.
18. *Feeling into Words*, p. 60.
19. *The Sense of Place*, pp. 137, 149.
20. *Feeling into Words*, p. 56.
21. *The Sense of Place*, pp. 141, 141.
22. *Feeling into Words*, pp. 54, 55.
23. *Mossbawn*, p. 19.
24. *Feeling into Words*, p. 54.
25. Ibid., p. 55.
26. *The God in the Tree*, pp. 183, 186, 184, 186.
27. *The Sense of Place*, pp. 132, 133, 134.
28. *The God in the Tree*, p. 186.
29. *The Sense of Place*, p. 134.
30. *The God in the Tree*, p. 186.
31. Ibid., p. 189.
32. Ibid., p. 183.
33. *The Sense of Place*, p. 135.

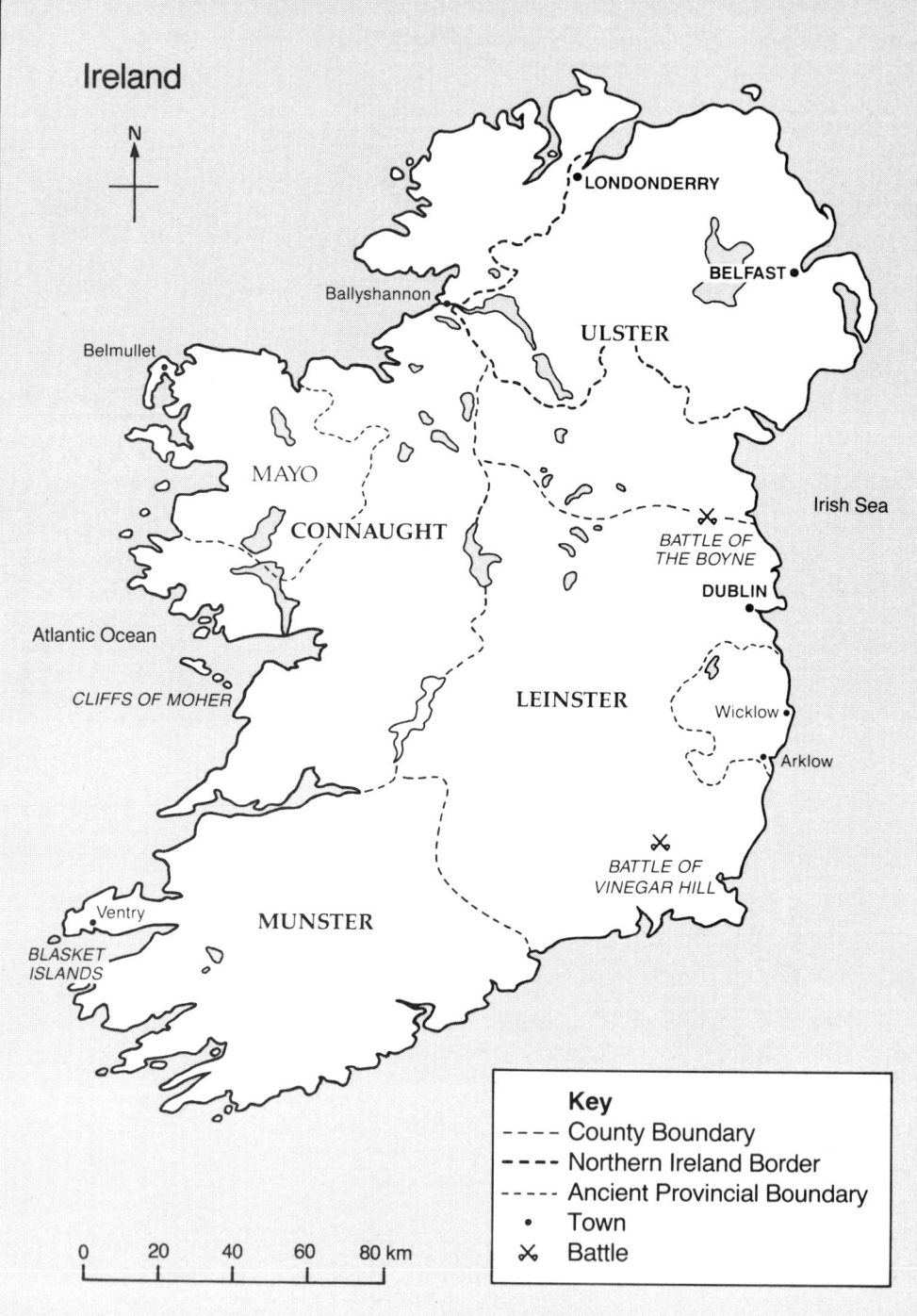

Seamus Heaney at home in Dublin, 1978.

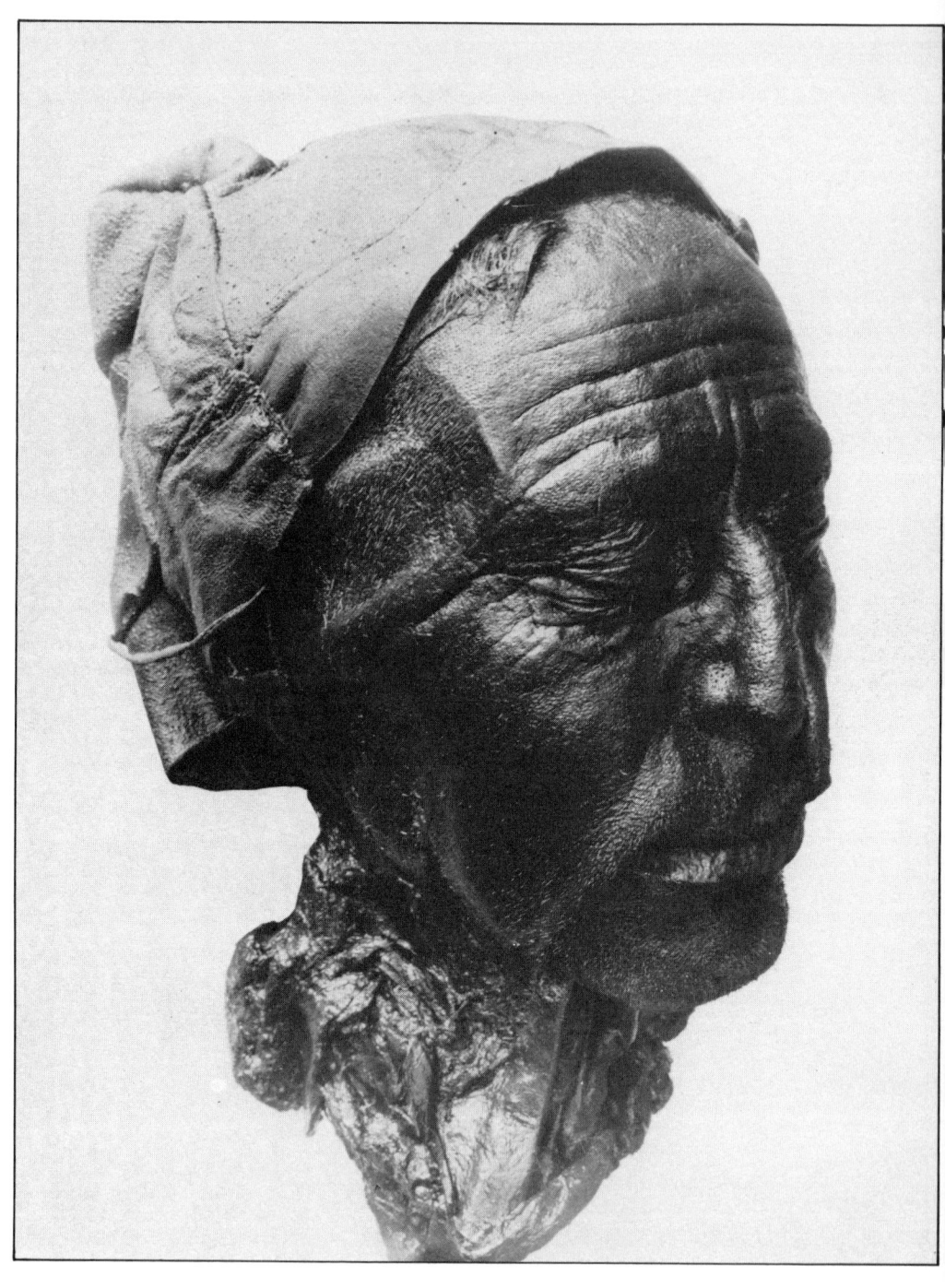

The head of the Tollund man. The whole body was discovered preserved in peat at Tollund, Jutland, Denmark, on 8th May, 1950.

Storing potatoes in a 'pit'. This traditional method of storing the potato crop is still in use.

Lough Neagh Eels. Images of the eels and fishing are used in earlier work such as *A Lough Neagh Sequence* and again in *Viking Dublin: Trial Pieces*.

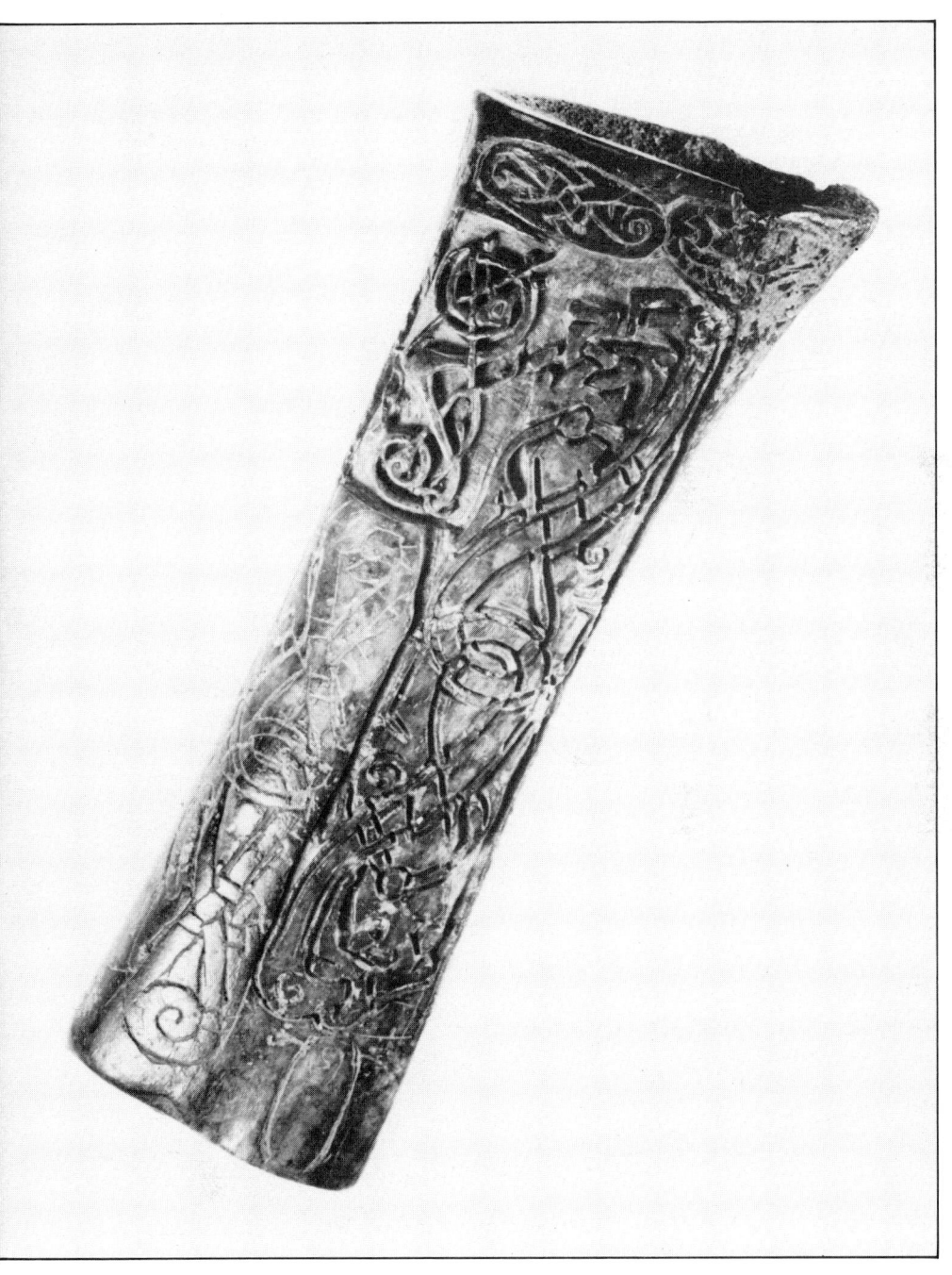

A bone trial piece, with carving in the Irish Scandinavian Rigerike style, found in the course of National Museum of Ireland excavations of old Dublin.

Chapter Three

'Wintering Out'

Political events in Ulster: 1963–1972

Seamus Heaney's poetic career has been shadowed by political events in Ulster. When **Death of a Naturalist** appeared in 1966, the Province was experiencing a new and tragically short-lived period of hope. The I.R.A. campaign launched against "British imperialism"[1] in 1956 had been contained. In 1963, Sean Lemass, Prime Minister of the Irish Republic, took the unprecedented step of acknowledging the Government of Northern Ireland and followed this gesture of conciliation with a visit to his Ulster counterpart, Captain Terence O'Neill, at Stormont in 1965. O'Neill also made an effort, as Heaney himself puts it, "to promote a gradual healing of the sectarian sores in the politics of Ulster" by urging the controlling Protestant Unionist Party to initiate a number of cautious reforms which might go some way towards answering the grievances of the Catholic population: "unemployment, lack of housing, discrimination in jobs and gerrymandering in electoral affairs".[2]

By 1969, the year of **Door into the Dark**, these signs of hope had gone. Encouraged by O'Neill's overtures, by the success of Civil Rights campaigners in America, and by the protest movements of France and Germany, the Catholics of Ulster began to demand far-reaching reforms. Matters came to a head on 24th August 1968 when, following the eviction of a Catholic squatter family and the allocation of their house to a young Protestant girl by the local government of Dungannon, County Tyrone, the Catholic population organized a march to demand redress. An attempt to hold a second march, in Londonderry, was opposed by William Craig, Unionist Minister of Home Affairs, on the grounds that it might provoke Protestant retaliation. When the marchers attempted to defy Craig's ban, on 5th October, they were forcibly dispersed by the police. As a reaction to this use of force, a protest movement was formed at Queen's University Belfast, from which emerged the political pressure group known as the "People's Democracy".

Sectarian tension escalated dramatically on 4th January 1969 when, at Burntollet Bridge outside Londonderry, a "People's Democracy" march was attacked by Protestants – about half of whom were later identified as members of the "B Specials", the Ulster Special Constabulary – wielding "iron bars and nailstudded coshes".[3] The anti-Catholic backlash had begun. On 28th April, the reformist O'Neill, having lost the support of his party, resigned; and in the week of 12th August to 19th August, severe sectarian conflict in Londonderry's Bogside and Belfast's Divis Street resulted in the deaths of two Catholics, shot by Royal Ulster Constabulary policemen using Browning guns mounted on armoured cars.

British troops were sent in to Ulster on 13th August to keep the peace, but could do nothing to prevent a hardening of attitudes on both sides. Ian Paisley began to mobilize extreme Protestant opinion against the Civil Rights movement while in November, Sean McStiofain set up a breakaway "Provisional Army Council" of the I.R.A. which denounced the "Official" I.R.A.'s failure to defend the Catholic population during the August riots, and which determined to resume the armed struggle for the "thirty-two county Irish Republic proclaimed at Easter, 1916".[4]

By the time Heaney's third volume, **Wintering Out**, was published in 1972, the violence of Ulster was drawing to a terrible climax. The British Army's use of "CS" gas to control a Catholic riot on the Ballymurphy estate in Belfast in April 1970; the Stormont Government's decision in August 1971 to arrest and intern indefinitely without trial Catholics suspected of terrorism; the killing of thirteen Catholic civilians by British paratroops during the "Bloody Sunday" Civil Rights march in Londonderry on 30th January 1972, all helped to inflame the Catholic population and increase support for the Provisional I.R.A. In the seven months from May to December 1970 alone, membership of the Provisionals rose from 100 to eight times that number. Once again, attempts to reconcile the Catholics provoked a Protestant reaction. When the British Prime Minister, Edward Heath, abolished the Stormont Parliament on 24th March 1972 and established William Whitelaw as Secretary for Ulster, the Ulster Defence Force, a Protestant paramilitary organization, swelled its numbers to some 30,000, set up barricades around those areas of Belfast under its control, and defied the British Army in open confrontation. On both sides of the sectarian divide, atrocity was countered by atrocity. By the end of 1972, Lord Windlesham could report that:

> a total of 8,223 people, or about one in every 200 of the population, has directly suffered death or personal injury from the campaign of violence in Northern Ireland in less than two years.[5]

Heaney's response to the situation in Ulster

Throughout this period, Heaney observed events in his homeland with a sense of professional concern, for one of the tasks he undertook at this time was to write occasional articles about life in Ulster for London-based magazines like **The Listener** and **The New**

Statesman. The tone of the earliest of these pieces is that of an urbane journalist who wishes to present his educated, English audience with an objective if somewhat bemused account of strange folk rituals in an outlying province. Writing in the summer of 1966, Heaney describing Belfast as "essentially a country town", noted that "Many of the people here rely for their identity on their adopted political allegiance rather than their geographical position", and explains, with a detail which assumes ignorance on the part of his readers, the significance of the Protestant marches on 12th July.

A sense of tension can be detected even in this early article. On the one hand, Heaney seems to want to appear blasé about the problems of his homeland – as though he feels slightly ashamed that a contributor to sophisticated English magazines should be associated with a quarrel which, in 1966, must have seemed ludicrously anachronistic. Viewed with hindsight, the comments generated by this attitude seem bitterly ironic now. Writing about the Catholic population's response to the Protestant marches of 12th July, Heaney observes:

> They console themselves with the fact that this annual belligerence is a sign of their own power; when they see Unionist politicians consorting with the Orange Order, they are happy simply to constitute a threat to the *status quo*.

However, this same article takes the threat of renewed sectarian violence very seriously indeed and is grimly prophetic:

> The atmosphere of the Troubles has been growing: there have been stabbings, shootings and bomb-throwings. A month ago it was still possible to say "hooliganism", but with the shooting down of three youths on Sunday and the death of one of them nobody can ignore the threat to public safety.[6]

As the crisis deepened, so Heaney's journalistic stance changed. The police action of 5th October 1968 "shocked moderate opinion on all sides" and shook him off the political fence. "Up until then," he wrote in an article published in **The Listener** on 24th October, "a Catholic might believe in shades of grey." Now, however, Heaney used his access to an influential English audience not only to condemn the "brutal control" exercised by the police and the "bland indifference of Mr Craig", but also to present the Catholic case and list the six demands of the "People's Democracy".

In the heady days of 1968, when the "new 'Londonderry Air'"

sounded "very like 'We shall overcome'" and Queen's University seemed to rival Paris or Berkeley as a forcing-house of exhilerating political change, it was possible for Heaney to assert that:

> the Catholic minority in Northern Ireland at large, if it is to retain any self-respect, will have to risk the charge of wrecking the new moderation and seek justice more vociferously.[7]

But when that moderation actually was wrecked, by violence two months later, Heaney was taken aback. "I did not realise at the time", he observes in his account of *Requiem for the Croppies* from **Door into the Dark**, "that the original heraldic murderous encounter between Protestant yeoman and Catholic rebel was to be initiated again in the summer of 1969, in Belfast, two months after the book was published".[8]

As the violence worsened, Heaney's initial sense of uncertainty gradually reasserted itself and grew into disillusionment. A visit in autumn 1970 to the supposed hub of radical activity, the University of California, tempered his faith in student politics when he discovered that "While Berkeley shouts, Belfast burns". Exiled among what he now regarded as a "rip-off generation", the cult phrases of youthful revolution evoked despair rather than challenge when applied to his home: "But, hopelessly," he writes from America, "Ireland is where the action is."[9] Back in Belfast for the Christmas following the introduction of internment, Heaney wrote of "weary twisted emotions that are rolled like a ball of hooks and sinkers in the heart" and confessed that the problem of Ulster now left him "fatigued by a continuous adjudication between agony and injustice".[10] By the July of 1972, he had abandoned the North for life in the Irish Republic.

A sense of divided loyalty

What transformed the campaigning journalist of 1968 into the war-weary refugee of 1972 was something much deeper and complex than political disillusionment or a sense of revulsion against "the fury of Irish Republicanism".[11] At the core of Heaney's relationship with Ulster lay a profound sense of conflict and divided loyalty. Nowhere does this feeling of "cultural schizophrenia"[12] reveal itself more strongly than in his attitude towards the country which had brought Protestant Northern Ireland into being. Heaney owed a great debt to England: its lecturers had taught him, its publishers printed his poems and essays, he moved in its literary circles. Moreover, from the time when English comics had "opened" upon his childhood "like magic casements",[13] that "literary awareness" which was to become "his life" had been "nourished"[14] by the language. An English poet, Gerard Manley Hopkins, had inspired the young Heaney with "the desire to write";[15] he made his living by teaching English literature; his poetic concerns were those of his major English contemporaries.[16]

And yet, English was spoken also by "the voices of ... education"[17] whose "'poertry'" had threatened to separate Heaney from his childhood roots. More than this, it was the language of a people who had conquered and colonised Ireland: to speak the conqueror's language was to acknowledge defeat, and to speak it with the accent of a "South Derry" Catholic was, as the poet recalls in *The Ministry of Fear*, to invite hostility and contempt.[18] But perhaps the most serious charge to be laid against English was the fact that it destroyed the native Catholic people's sense of "belonging to a place, an ancestry, a history, a culture"[19] by denying them access to their ancient Gaelic heritage and thus transforming the Irish landscape into "a manuscript" which they had "lost the skill to read". How could the native people of Ireland achieve that "nourishment which springs from knowing and belonging to a certain place and a certain mode of life"[20] – so vital, in Heaney's view, for the preservation of local identity against the threat of a global materialistic ideology – if they could no longer speak the language which had named and thus defined the villages, fields and loughs of their world?

A sense of moral dilemma also conditioned Heaney's response to the crisis in Ulster. The Catholic in him was "swung ... by the long tail of race and resentment".[21] Like other Ulstermen of his religion, he had known what it felt like to be told "'Catholics, in general, don't speak/As well as students from the Protestant schools'";[22] he too had been stopped arbitrarily on the road at night and searched by police with sten-guns, because the mere mention of his Christian name had marked him at once as a member of a subservient and potentially hostile tribe.

As a poet, Heaney felt the Catholic Ulsterman's sense of cultural dislocation particularly keenly, for the English supremacy had cut him off from the Gaelic poetic tradition which should have been his birthright. It was for these reasons that Heaney could confess to finding the "destructive elements" which were "in the air" of Belfast in that critical year of 1972 "deeply exhilerating"[23] – why should the whole rotten edifice of Protestant power not be pulled down?

And yet, again, those voices of education called him in a

completely different direction. Whether he liked it or not, he had been brought up in, and now made his living from promoting, a cultural system which advocated "humane love and reason". How could he, a poet and man of letters, feel anything but "pity and terror" for those – both Catholic and Protestant – whose lives were being "shattered blandly or terribly" by bombing, shooting or internment? As if Heaney's attitude towards the Ulster crisis was not complicated enough, a feeling of guilt clouded the issue even further. Protected from the sufferings of his countrymen by a good job and a house in a relatively safe neighbourhood, he felt a sense of shame because the violence was happening elsewhere:

> We live in the sickly light of TV screens, with a pane of selfishness between ourselves and the suffering. We survive explosions and funerals and live on among the families of the victims, those blown apart and those in cells apart.[24]

Just as Heaney the Catholic citizen and university lecturer felt equivocal in his response to the situation in Ulster, so Heaney the artist was reluctant to take up the mantle of "Poet of the Troubles". For a writer who regarded the process of composition as a "kind of somnambulist encounter", who "listened for poems" as carefully and patiently as a water-diviner might feel for water, the thought of producing instant, journalistic verse in a kind of knee-jerk reaction to the latest political development was totally unacceptable:

> It would wrench the rhythms of my writing procedures to start squaring up to contemporary events with more will than ways to deal with them.[25]

With his profound belief in the mystery of the poet's craft, Heaney could never allow his art to become merely "a diagram of political attitudes."[26] Besides, to resort to the simplicity of the diagram would be to invite a simplistic response from the critics, who might start to speak again of writers being "hurt" into "poetry" by "mad Ireland"[27] and stereotype his work as an "Exhibition of the Good that can come out of Troubled Times."[28]

The poetic landscape of 'Wintering Out'

Despite all these hesitations, Heaney could not ignore the crisis in Ulster which **Door into the Dark** had come too early to examine.

The title of his new book shows just how reluctant the poet felt about trying to succeed where the politicians had failed by offering specific, immediate answers to ancient problems. Where **Door into the Dark** speaks of exhilerating movement, **Wintering Out** offers entrenchment and endurance. The atmosphere of this third volume is as cold and bleak as the title suggests. The landscape of **Door into the Dark** is bathed in sunshine or echoes to the sound of running water and the tools of mythically powerful craftsmen, but **Wintering Out** reveals only "fog/on the lawn", "the tundra's whistling brush", fields "lost" to a flooded river, a "burnt-out gable".

The door into the dark has led "'back to no/oak groves'" of pantheistic vision, but to a dead-end where "mizzling rain/blurs the far end/of the cart track". And the darkness that once enticed the poet with its promise of mystery and revelation is now a place of miserable exile from which, as in the poem *Good-Night*, for example, he looks back longingly, like some hunted beast, to the "edged den of light" radiating from that farmhouse whose familiar safety he had deliberately turned away from and cannot now re-enter. **Wintering Out** is peopled by figures who have been left out in the now threatening darkness and who hover like ghosts on the edge of unattainable warmth, security and light. The "Bye-Child", locked in his hen-house prison, "Puts his eye to a chink" and stares with "puzzled love" at the glowing lamp in the "back window" of the farm. The "Servant Boy", a "jobber among shadows", moves furtively "through some outhouse" towards "the back doors of the little barons". The "Last Mummer" "pads up the terrace" "out of the fog/on the lawn" only to find himself excluded from the "charmed ... ring" of television watchers.

The fatalism of 'Wintering Out'

Keenly aware of the ambiguity of his own response to the Ulster crisis, the closest Heaney felt he could come to making some direct statement on the situation was to express this sense of being in the dark: of being – as he puts it at the end of his poem about the Tollund Man – "lost" and "unhappy". In an interview published in December 1972 Heaney, confessing that the mood of his new book of poems was pessimistic, held out only one small ray of hope. Commenting upon the title, he said:

> It is a phrase associated with cattle, and with hired boys also. In some ways, it links up with a very resonant line of English

verse that every schoolboy knows: "Now is the winter of our discontent." It is meant to gesture towards the distresses that we are all undergoing in this country at the minute. It is meant to be, I suppose, comfortless enough, but with a notion of survival in it.[29]

A "gesture", a "notion of survival" – this was the most Heaney felt able to offer in the year which began with "Bloody Sunday" and ended with the Provisional I.R.A. using Russian rocket-launchers against the British Army.

A poem which expresses this "notion of survival" in its most pragmatic form is *Servant Boy*, where Heaney implies that the present crisis is like "the back-end of a bad year": if the people of Ulster could only grit their teeth and succeed in "wintering out" the difficult season then surely, as he had already anxiously anticipated in December 1970, "Something must give".[30] Until that time, people of good will must lie low and keep out of trouble, preserving as best they can the "warm eggs" of civilized behaviour. Throughout his third volume of poetry, Heaney presents figures who have done this successfully. The mummer, for example, though "trammelled/in the taboos of the country", is too wily to take sides and thus risk his life. Instead, he survives by "picking a nice way through/the long toils of blood/and feuding." The servant boy himself is praised because, as Heaney tells him, you "kept your patience/and your counsel"; while in *Gifts of Rain*, the creature who survives the "Cloudburst and steady downpour" is the one who can "sense weather/by his skin" and "fords/his life by sounding" – carefully testing the water's depth before committing himself to movement. There is nothing positive about the advice that Heaney offers here. His stance is defensive and his attitude fatalistic. It is as though he feels that the spirit of violence raised on 5th October 1968 must run its course. Those who did not want to be hurt by it would have to try and keep out of the way. **Wintering Out** offers scant comfort to the relatives of those killed or injured in the "Abercorn" restaurant bombing, or to "the dependants of the internees in Long Kesh camp".[31]

Though some might have felt disappointed by the negative response to the Ulster crisis expressed in **Wintering Out**, it should have surprised nobody who had read Heaney's second volume. The reason why he felt so fatalistic about events in the province since October 1968 was because they confirmed, horribly, that dark vision of Irish history which he had begun to explore in **Door into the Dark**. Once again, it seemed, the cycle had come round to communal violence. Searching, in *Bog Oak*, for some sign that might guide him beyond the "cart track" whose "softening ruts" seem to lead nowhere, the poet's gaze is drawn, not to the future, but back to the past, for the future and the past of Ireland seem to be one. The figures who "creep" before him "towards watercress and carrion" are those victims of the Elizabethan wars whose wretched condition the poet Edmund Spenser described in his **Veue of the Present State of Ireland** in 1596; yet now, as the ancient "fault" of religious hatred "is opening" again, they come out from their hiding-places to haunt twentieth-century Ulster. Heaney's comment in *Tinder* sums up the paradox of the Irish situation: "We face the tundra's whistling brush", he writes, "With new history".

The theme of haunting

The idea that the ghosts of Ireland's past have been brought back from the grave by this latest eruption of the age-old sectarian war is emphasised by the images of haunting which recur throughout **Wintering Out**. Always, the visitor is unwelcome, for he bears witness to some previous mistake or neglected duty, or else poses a question that his unwilling listener would rather not answer. Sometimes those who return come back from the dead. In *Limbo*, for example, the baby drowned by its mother exposes her secret act of murder to the whole community when he is "hauled in with the fish." Elsewhere, the living are haunted by the living. The "Last Mummer" hammers the bars of his irresponsible neighbours' gate because they have failed in their duty to perform the ancient folk-ritual of the mumming-play. The "Bye-Child" whom the woman had tried to lock out of her life will not go away but remains stubbornly "kennelled and faithful" until, released at last, his "remote mime" speaks more eloquently than any words could manage of sadism and "lunar distances/Travelled beyond love".

The poet, too, is a haunted man. No matter where he travels, he cannot shake off the feeling that, as he tells his wife in *Summer Home*, there is "something ... dogging us". In this particular poem, the "something" is a sense of guilt provoked by "her small lost weeping"; but the spectre of domestic conflict would be an almost welcome guest if it could only distract him from his real pursuers – the problems of Ireland which threatened to dominate his private and artistic life. Just as Edmund Spenser's efforts to forget about the Irish wars of his day were frustrated when "the rebels ... threw him out of house and home",[32] so Heaney's attempts to escape the claims of sectarian Ulster are consistently thwarted.

The themes of love and nature

In **Wintering Out** Heaney made a determined effort to break fresh poetic ground. Indeed one of the ways in which his publishers Faber and Faber tried to sell the new book was by praising it for representing "a noticeable widening of his poetic landscapes."[33] Yet, try as Heaney might to go his own way artistically by writing about important new areas of personal (and potentially healing) experience such as his marriage, he could not break free from the influence of events in Ulster. Even works which examine supposedly positive aspects of married life – the wedding day, foreign travel, the rearing of a young family – offer symbols of conflict, suffering, ritualised remorse.

Thus the poem *Wedding Day* opens with the curt and unexpected statement "I am afraid", and proceeds like a surreal silent film through a sequence of nightmarish images and frightened, unspoken questions which culminate in confused flight. In *Summer Home* the act of reconciliation after a quarrel is portrayed, not in terms of tender intimacy, but formally, as though it were a religious ceremony. The simply beauty of "wild cherry and rhododendron" wilts beneath an unsupportable symbolic pressure when the poet loads the flowers with penitential religious significance. Even the physical act of love, which is meant to seal that reconciliation, is described as an almost unendurably painful but necessary surgical operation. When it is over, man and wife lie, not in peace, but "as if the cold flat of a blade/had winded us". The achievements won by love in these poems amount to little: the most the poet can offer at the end of *Serenades* is a resolution to be patient next time the children break his sleep.

If love offers no refuge for Heaney in **Wintering Out**, neither does nature. The pantheistic vision of **Door into the Dark** is absent from this third volume. What beauty there is, is perceived fitfully – out of the corner of the eye, perhaps, during a domestic quarrel. Thus in *Summer Home*, as the poet and his wife "lie stiff till dawn", he suddenly notices, briefly, how the vine "holds its filling burden to the light." Significantly, it is a foreign landscape which provides this image of abundance so at odds with his own unfruitful relationship. Back home in *Ireland*, Heaney's current definition of natural beauty in *Nerthus* contains none of the lushness of his earlier poems but is austere, rough and wind-swept: "an ash-fork staked in peat," "A seasoned, unsleeved taker of the weather". Living creatures delighted him in *At Ardboe Point* but in *Serenades* they arouse only indifference or mild hostility. The sedge-warbler is dismissed with a cliché as "A little bird with a big voice". Its "racket" of a song matches the "broken voice of a crow" or the "wheeze of bats" and irritates the poet by breaking his sleep.

All that repairing of Heaney's relationship with the natural world which took place in **Door into the Dark** seems to be undone. This relapse is demonstrated most clearly in *Shore Woman*, a work similar in style and theme to *Death of a Naturalist* and *The Wife's Tale* – two poems which represent the extremes of Heaney's response to the natural world. Superficially, *Shore Woman* and *The Wife's Tale* are very similar. Both poems are narrated by country women who recount, in four paragraphs of decasyllabic blank verse, an incident from work shared with their husbands. *The Wife's Tale* presents an unhurried, tranquil picture of marital harmony and sunlit agricultural prosperity, but *Shore Woman* like *Summer Home* portrays a couple who are alienated from each other and sets their story against a dramatically dark and gaunt seascape in which death comes suddenly and treacherously, for man as for fish, beneath the cold light of the moon.

Leaving the idyllic pastoral of *The Wife's Tale* far behind, *Shore Woman* recreates that nightmare vision of nature as the punisher of human transgression first evoked in *Death of a Naturalist*. The Lough Neagh fishermen would understand exactly why husband and wife in this poem suffer the retribution of the porpoises' attack: not only did they take the mackerel too easily, but the husband then compounded their crime by sneering at his wife's respect for the natural world. They pay for their actions by having to witness a revelation of nature's power more frightening than anything seen at the flax-dam. In a voice powerfully reminiscent of Robert Lowell,[34] Heaney describes the woman cowering at the mercy of the porpoises:

> I lay and screamed
> under splashed brine in an open rocking boat
> Feeling each dunt and slither through the timber,
> Sick at their huge pleasures in the water.

"Befitting emblems of adversity": Heaney's response to the crisis in Ulster in 'Wintering Out'

Edmund Spenser tried to escape from the Irish wars of his day by "dreaming sunlight" in the security of his estate at Kilcolman.

Seamus Heaney sought refuge from the twentieth-century manifestation of those same wars by taking his family to California and trying to write about love and nature. But neither poet could free themselves from Ireland: Heaney's description of Christmas at Berkeley, written for **The Listener** in December 1970, is drawn inevitably back to thoughts of Belfast.[35] "Six thousand miles away" from home he either dreams wistfully of a peaceful Ulster's "untroubled dust" as in *Westering*, or is pursued by a nightmare vision of the Province:

> I remembered a dream that I'd had last year in California. I was shaving at the mirror of the bathroom when I glimpsed in the mirror a wounded man falling towards me with his bloodied hands lifted to tear at me or to implore.

In his poem *Oracle*, Heaney returns to a theme which obsesses him: the idea of being called away against his will from some natural hiding place in a field or a tree by voices from the outside world. In **Wintering Out** he is called from his nature poetry and his love poetry by the haunting faces and "bloodied hands" of all those who are being sucked into "the old vortex"[36] of sectarian violence: by the "needy" huddled in a "burnt-out gable"; by the thought of that "Bye-Child" whose image lies "like a rodent" on the "floor" of the poet's mind and whose "gaping wordless proof" of extreme human cruelty seems to bear mute witness to all the inhuman acts perpetrated in the name of Irish Christianity. "What do I say", Heaney asks as he gazes at his suffering countrymen in *Stump*, "if they wheel out their dead?" In the face of such misery, nature poetry and poems about the love of individuals seem self-indulgent, irrelevant. When two tribes are trying to destroy each other, "love calls tiny as a tuning fork" or shrinks to nothing more than "a skewered heart/And a legend of love" scrawled on a toilet wall. As Heaney confesses to his wife in *Roots*, "The touch of love" grows "helpless" in the "old Gomorrah" of cursed Belfast. It is little wonder that the poet felt obliged to relegate the poems which deal with love and nature in **Wintering Out** to a short second section of their own.

The split structure of this third volume of verse symbolizes the tensions which inform it. Writing about the concerns of three earlier, Protestant Ulster poets, Heaney describes a feeling of dual identity and a sense of poetic obligation which is also his own:

> All three men were born to a sense of "two nations" and part of their imaginative effort was a solving of their feelings towards

Ireland, a new answer to the question ... "What is my nation?"[37]

It is significant that *A Northern Hoard*, the sequence of poems from **Wintering Out** which makes most direct mention of the current situation in Ulster, quotes as its epigraph lines 131 and 132 of Coleridge's *Rime of the Ancient Mariner*; for Heaney's relationship with Ireland, demanding as it did a creative response to those questions about personal and national identity, burdened him as heavily as the albatross hung round the Mariner's neck. If he were to take up his homeland's challenge, it would be with that sense of reluctance almost akin to loathing expressed in the weary opening line of *Stump*: "I am riding to plague again."

Heaney the journalist might feel able gradually to tone down his contribution to the political debate about Ulster, and even, eventually, to excuse himself from it; but for Heaney the poet there could be no such easy way out. Whether he liked it or not, he would always remain "a black stump of home", bound to the sufferings of his people by what in *Gifts of Rain* he terms "the shared calling of blood". But more than this, Heaney had brought the obligation to write about Ireland upon himself in **Door into the Dark** when he had begun to explore the role of poet as national or tribal spokesman, as *Vates* or *Diviner* – one who possessed "a gift for mediating between the latent resource and the community that wants it current and released". If the latent resource which the community wanted released was sectarian conflict, then the *Vates* had a duty to comply, preserving his poetic integrity as best he could. Looking back at **Wintering Out** two years after its publication, Heaney admits that he had no option but to acquiesce; for like the farmer in *Gifts of Rain*, he is "hooped to where he planted":

> I felt it imperative to discover a field of force in which, without abandoning fidelity to the processes and experience of poetry as I have outlined them, it would be possible to encompass the perspectives of a humane reason and at the same time to grant the religious intensity of the violence its deplorable authenticity and complexity.[38]

Heaney found the "field of force" he was looking for in the "answering Irish myth" which he had begun to explore in **Door into the Dark**. In that second volume, he had laid claim to the title of spokesman for the working people of rural Ireland and had tried to foster and assert their sense of communal identity as a means by which his homeland might maintain its cultural independence. Now, as the Ulster crisis deepened, he turned again to these people for inspiration but this time he came, not as a spokesman, but as someone looking for help.

Maintaining "fidelity" to his view of poetry as "divination and revelation"[39] of *les vers donnés*, Heaney becomes a "hoarder of common ground", an "inquisitor" of Ireland's "possessed air". Like the diviner of his analogy, he listens for an answer. Sometimes it comes from a living member of the rural community such as that "chance vestal daughter" of Derrygarve whose words inspire the poet to a renewed faith in the Irish language in *A New Song*; but it is more accurate to describe Heaney's role here as that of a medium rather than a diviner, for it is, once more, by exploring his people's past that he hopes to find a solution to Ireland's problems. Heaney symbolizes this idea in **Wintering Out** by presenting images of the poet as someone who is trying to raise the dead – as though to find benign spirits who might counter the malevolent forces set free by the violence of October 1968. Thus in *Bog Oak*, standing amid the ruins of a cottage that the thatcher from **Door into the Dark** could have worked on, he ponders how he "might tarry/with the moustached/dead" – those "creel-fillers", perhaps, whose descendants he had described in *At a Potato Digging*. In *Gifts of Rain*, again he waits at a familiar childhood spot beside the rain-swollen Moyola, straining to question the "Soft voices of the dead" which he can almost hear beneath the noise of the flooded river, "whispering by the shore".

Elsewhere, Heaney plays upon his idea of composition as "a kind of somnambulist encounter" by creating an atmosphere of trance or vision in order to make poetic contact with the past. As the epigraph to *A Northern Hoard* suggests, he, like the sailors in Coleridge's poem, is "assured" by "dreams" of "the Spirit" that "plagued" the people of Ireland. "I'll dream it for us before dawn", Heaney tells his wife in *Roots*, as he attempts to make sense of "gunshot, siren and clucking gas". Again, in *The Last Mummer*, the consolation offered in the poem's final section can only be reached by dreaming about it.

The insights which Heaney achieves through these poems of seance or trance serve not only to confirm his vision of Irish history as cyclical, but also to validate that idea of the "answering Irish myth" explored in **Door into the Dark**. What could offer clearer proof of the fact that the Irish are a nation haunted by the ghosts of their past and bound to the land in a seemingly endless sacrificial process, than the knowledge that the working people of Ulster were prepared to murder each other for the sake of a quarrel at least four hundred years old?

In the bombings and the shootings Heaney saw the fulfilment of all that his second volume had foreseen. This sense of having been proved right made him more convinced than ever that the only positive contribution he as tribal poet could make to the current Ulster crisis, was to take his people to the heart of the Irish myth and show them the precise nature of the forces whose violence dominated their lives. If those forces could be understood, they might also be controlled. To the critics who asked what use poetry might be in a society shattered by violence, Heaney now had his answer:

> The question, as ever, is "How with this rage shall beauty hold a plea?" And my answer is, by offering "befitting emblems of adversity".[40]

The inadequacy of christian emblems

Clearly, the "emblem" of the crucified Christ, regarded for so long as the dominant symbol of Christian Ireland, would no longer suffice. As Heaney observed in 1974, the "psychology and mythologies implicit in the terms Irish Catholic and Ulster Protestant" were now "bankrupt".[41] How could anyone seriously use the word "Christian" to describe the atrocities being perpetrated by both sides in what was really little short of a tribal war? Moreover, for a religion that claimed brotherly love as its principal tenet, Christianity had not only failed to bring peace to Ireland, but had actually made matters worse by turning neighbour against neighbour.

It is because Heaney feels that Christianity is at best irrelevant and at worst a force for harm in Ulster that he rarely refers to it in **Wintering Out**; and when he does, he portrays it negatively. In *The Other Side*, for example, the bible is described, not as something which unites the Catholic and Protestant neighbours, but as a means by which the latter asserts his cultural and political superiority over the former. Sharing so much else in common, the two farmers cannot worship together: that "moan of prayers" coming from the Catholics" kitchen in Part III keeps the Protestant waiting "shyly" in the darkness, as though to discourage his tentative offer of friendship.

Elsewhere, Christianity is described as ineffectual, unable, in *Limbo*, to save the soul of the "small one thrown back/To the waters." "Even Christ's palms, unhealed," Heaney writes, "Smart and cannot fish there." The poet's attitude to the religion of his birth is summed up in *Westering*, the final poem of the collection. Here, in ironic contrast to the piety of John Donne's *Goodfriday, 1613. Riding Westward*, Heaney's flight to "The empty amphitheatre/Of the west" is presented as a "free fall", an exhilerating escape from that Catholicism whose spiritual claustrophobia and moral inertia are symbolized by empty streets and the depressing sound of "clappers" smacking "On a bare altar". Only in this poem does Heaney recapture the joyful sense of movement so evident in **Door into the Dark**: while others, locked into the old, stultifying system of belief, are "bent" before "the studded crucifix" of their imprisoned god on a day of penance and sorrow, he celebrates his new-found sense of liberation in a simile of exquisite and familiar delicacy:

> Roads unreeled, unreeled
>
> Falling light as casts
> Laid down
> On shining waters.

Christianity would not do because, like the *Bye-Child*, Ireland had travelled "lunar distances" beyond the concept of Christian love. As Heaney puts it in *Gifts of Rain*, the "shared calling of blood" provoked a need, not for Christ's teachings, but for "antediluvian lore". Only by reaching back further into that "world older and darker and greener than the world of early Christian Ireland", first explored in **Door into the Dark**, could the poet hope to find "befitting emblems of adversity" capable of encompassing those violent, pre-Christian forces which had for centuries brought suffering to his homeland.

The emblem of the Tollund Man and the magical world-view of 'Wintering Out'

Just when Heaney was beginning to search for these "emblems", he found exactly what he was looking for in a book written by a Danish Professor of Archaeology. Noting the significance of its title – **The Bog People** – and the fact that the English translation of the work appeared in 1969, "the year the killing started", Heaney's description of the book's subject explains just exactly why he found it so important:

> It was chiefly concerned with preserved bodies of men and women found in the bogs of Jutland, naked, strangled or with their throats cut, disposed under the peat since early Iron Age times. The author, P.V. Glob, argues convincingly that a number of these, and in particular the Tollund Man, whose head is now preserved near Aarhus in the museum at Silkeburg, were ritual sacrifices to the Mother Goddess, the goddess of the ground who needed new bridegrooms each winter to bed with her in her sacred place, in the bog, to ensure the renewal and fertility of the territory in the spring.[42]

Glob's book brought all Heaney's preoccupations together in one stunning poetic image of "unique haunting power"[43] and offered proof of everything he had said about the "Irish myth" in **Door into the Dark**. Those "unforgettable photographs" of the Tollund Man particularly, gave spectacular evidence that the bog was, literally a preserver of history and a territory haunted by unwelcome ghosts. More than this, they confirmed Heaney's vision, first expressed in *At a Potato Digging*, of the landscape as a "black/Mother" – a cruel, pagan goddess who demanded human sacrifice in return for a successful harvest. Heaney regarded the Tollund Man with the same sense of awe with which a believer might look at the Turin Shroud. In the face of that victim sacrificed to a religion much older and darker than Christianity, he found the befitting emblem of adversity he needed to replace the inadequate symbol of the crucified Christ. The potency and the relevance of this emblem were enhanced for Heaney by the knowledge that "the severed human head" was "a kind of shorthand symbol for the entire religious outlook of the pagan Celts". The image of this "martyr" blended in the poet's mind with "photographs of atrocities, past and present, in the long rites of Irish political and religious struggles"; and the "goddess of the ground" which had claimed his life came to represent the goddess of territory – "Mother Ireland". Suddenly, Heaney had found the poetic metaphor he wanted in order to understand and thus to control his experience of the Ulster crisis. The inspiration struck him with a feeling of religious intensity:

> When I wrote this poem, I had a completely new sensation, one of fear. It was a vow to go on pilgrimage and I felt as it came to me – and again it came quickly – that unless I was

deeply in earnest about what I was saying, I was simply invoking dangers for myself. It is called *The Tollund Man*.[44]

The Tollund Man offers the most radical and complex statement made in **Wintering Out** about the renewal of sectarian violence in Ireland. By comparing modern Ulster to "the old man-killing parishes" of Jutland, Heaney places the current crisis in a timeless, mythological context; and he tries to make sense of the present-day killings by setting them along side the deaths of the *Croppies*, the Lough Neagh fishermen, and the famine victims of 1845, as yet more "ritual sacrifices to the Mother Goddess". Invoking the Tollund Man as the "archetypal pattern" of such sacrifice, addressing "Him" (the capital "H" is significant) as though he was a benign deity who might counter the black magic stirred by "the cauldron bog", the poet calls upon this true patron saint of Ireland to do what neither Patrick nor Christ have been able to do – "to make germinate" the "Flesh of labourers" and the "Stockinged corpses", so that their deaths might provide the seeds from which the harvest of true peace could grow.

Heaney knew that the bleak vision of the Ulster crisis presented in *The Tollund Man* would seem "remote from the agnostic world of economic interest",[45] but it came from the heart of his people's mythology, and belonged to that Yeatsian "counter-cultural movement"[46] and "magical world-view"[47] with which, as tribal poet, he had allied himself in **Door into the Dark**. In *The Tollund Man*, Heaney felt that he touched the problems of Ireland at their nerve-centre. He would not betray his vision for, as he argued, that vision was "not remote from the psychology of the Irishmen and Ulstermen who do the killing".[48]

Far from playing down this "magical world-view" of the Ulster crisis in **Wintering Out**, Heaney emphasises it. The Tollund Man is only one among several figures from the mythical world of "country customs and beliefs"[49] who are invoked to counter the power of the "cauldron bog". Since Heaney sees strife-torn Ulster as a land frozen in the grip of a political and spiritual winter, he uses the folk ritual of first-footing. This custom by which the first person to cross the threshold at New Year brings good luck for the coming twelve months symbolizes his belief that only by rediscovering their cultural roots can the Irish people hope to find a way forward out of the impasse.

In each case, the act of first-footing is carried out by a figure who represents that folk culture in its most mysterious and magical form. In *Servant Boy* it is performed by the "Old work-whore", that most humble and oppressed member of rural Irish society who has nothing but his culture to sustain him. In *The Last Mummer*, the first-footers are those "Christmas rhymers"[50] whose mumming play about the sacrifice and eventual triumph of Good over Evil represents a dim, twentieth-century memory of the ancient religious faith which martyred the Tollund Man. Heaney knows that there is little chance that what he calls the "reliable citizen"[51] of modern Ulster will make the imaginative effort needed to understand this "magical world-view", and so he describes the first-footers as figures who are shrouded in darkness or just beyond reach. The servant boy, "a jobber among shadows", is glimpsed momentarily, "swinging a hurricane-lamp/through some outhouse"; the mummers appear in a dream, or are perhaps just seen "disappearing beyond the lamplit/slabs of a yard".

Whether attainable or not, there is no doubt about the religious identity of this vision. As in *The Tollund Man* so again in *The Last Mummer*, the Catholic Heaney risks "blasphemy" by repossessing the most sacred symbols of his childhood faith in the name of a far older religion. When the mummer makes "dark tracks" into the New Year, the poet takes the image of the "monstrance" in which Catholics display the Blessed Sacrament and fills it, not with the consecrated wafer, but with the "moon's host". In *Westering* it is the moon again rather than the "studded crucifix" which bears the "stigmata" of Christ's five wounds.

This elevation of the feminine symbol of the moon as a religious emblem serves to emphasise the power which "Mother Ireland" holds over the country. Her freshly aroused desire for sacrifice is further suggested in **Wintering Out** by Heaney's portrayal of a series of magical or mysterious women whose cruelty or indifference counters the benign masculine power of servant boy, mummer and Tollund Man. There is, of course, the "goddess" herself who, fatally, "tightened her torc" upon her "Bridegroom"; but this act of violence is repeated by the mother in *Limbo* who drowns her baby and the woman in *Bye-Child* who tortures a boy by imprisoning him in a henhouse. Elsewhere the act of rejection is less extreme but no less complete: the "Shore Woman" walks the beach at night "to get away from him/Skittering his spit across the stove"; the mermaid of *Maighdean Mara* deserts her human children; even the woman in *Good-Night* "cancels everything behind her" as she steps into the "honeyed corridor" and abandons her observer to the darkness.

The theme of language

Wintering Out is a bleak work, concerned with holding on, enduring, looking inward. One of the results of this increased sense of introversion is the inclusion in the book of a number of poems which actually examine the poet's stock-in-trade itself: language. In his treatment of this theme, as elsewhere throughout the third volume, Heaney is pulled two ways. The Irish Catholic in him, excited by the political atmosphere of Berkeley in 1970-1, felt an "awareness that poetry was a force, almost a mode of power, certainly a mode of resistance".[52] A poet who wished to maintain "the perspectives of a humane reason" throughout the crisis might not be able to advocate armed struggle as a means of defending the claims of his tribe; but he could at least help to preserve their threatened sense of cultural identity, not only by giving them a myth with which to interpret their situation, but also by following Yeats in revealing how words themselves might be used to "bind the people of the Irish place to the body of their world".[53]

Heaney explains what he means by this in *Gifts of Rain*. Using the name of the Moyola River as an example, he describes how "the locale", the sense of place, is bedded in "the utterance", the word which names it. Heaney suggests that the river was given the name "Moyola" because this particular sound was the closest the human voice could come to imitating the noise made by the "tawny guttural water" which, literally, "spells itself". If the essence of river, mountain or village is captured in its name, and the Irish landscape was named by Irish speakers, how can their English speaking descendants possibly achieve that vital "felt knowledge of ... place"? Unable to read the manuscript of the Irish landscape, they are condemned to "go as tourists" in their own homeland, denied either a "sense of wonder or a sense of tradition".[54]

Heaney himself was deeply aware of this loss, for even in the name of his childhood home he found a "metaphor of the split culture of Ulster." The official, "Ordnance Survey spelling" of "Mossbawn" stamped it with an English identity as "the fortified farmhouse upon the bog"; but for the native Irish inhabitants of that farmhouse, the word was pronounced "Moss bann" and took on the older, Gaelic meaning of "the white moss, the moss of bog-cotton". Heaney felt that "the marks of English influence" – symbolized by their characteristic buildings, "the squared-off walls of bawn and demesne" – had "dropped on the country like the jaws of a man-trap".[55] To restore the native people's sense of place, the poet had to teach them how to read the Ulster landscape on Gaelic rather than English terms.

Heaney tries to do this by describing how his own response to places of personal significance was transformed once he had reached beneath the Anglicized version of their names to the "forgotten Gaelic music"[56] below. "Anahorish", for example, is the name of the townland where the poet attended primary school. To an English speaker, the word would reveal nothing; but for Heaney the knowledge that "Anahorish" is the Anglicized form of *anach fhior uisce*, "the place of clear water", charges it with a new meaning. How fitting for a poet who uses images of flowing water to symbolize poetic inspiration, that "the place of clear water" should also be the place where his own creativity was first directed into the channel of literature. Interpreted in this way, the word "Anahorish" becomes a metaphor of awakening innocence, discovery, adventure – a key with which potent memories can be unlocked. As long as he can say the name, the poet can summon up the spirit of Anahorish whenever he wants and thus preserve his sense of that place as "a country of the mind",[57] no matter what physical dangers may threaten the actual townland in years to come.

Only by rediscovering that "dying Irish language" which was "exhaled in … place-names"[58] could a native Ulsterman really appreciate just how deeply "locale" is bedded in "utterance". The knowledge that "Broagh" is the Anglicized form of *bruach* or "riverbank", for example, transforms the word vividly for the poet into a visual and aural image of wet earth. So powerfully does it work upon his imagination that he only has to look at the letter "o" of "Broagh" printed upon a page to recapture in his mind's eye the picture of a heelmark sinking into the riverbank's sodden "garden mould". Similarly in *Anahorish*: the "soft gradient" of that "first hill in the world" is represented by the short, rising nasal sound of the first two syllables, while the lush and level surface at the top "where springs washed into/the shiny grass" expands into "vowel-meadow" and sibilance.

In works like *Anahorish* and *Broagh*, Heaney is moving towards that genre of Irish poetry called *dinnseanchas*: "poems and tales which relate the original meanings of place names and constitute a form of mythological etymology".[59] And certainly, that part of his nature which responds to "the lure of the native experience"[60] or finds the events of 1972 "deeply exhilarating", is attracted to the idea of making a nationalistic, anti-British gesture of cultural independence in **Wintering Out** by championing the Irish language. This is the voice which, in *The Other Side*, rejects the Protestant neighbour's "tongue of chosen people" whose words are "too big for our small lanes"; prefaces the poem *Shore Woman* with a Gaelic proverb; dedicates *Maighdean Mara* to Seán O h-Eochaidh; or, more forcefully in *Traditions*, describes the silencing of Ireland's "guttural muse" by the "alliterative tradition" of English as an act of linguistic rape. It makes its most bold statement in *A New Song*, where Heaney declares that the native tongue "must" rise again like a river to "flood, with vowelling embrace", each of those colonists' "Demesnes" "staked out" in the "consonants" of the conqueror's language.

The Catholic nationalist in Heaney might speak with this voice, but the lecturer and poet who worked within and loved the English literary tradition could not. In two essays particularly, *Belfast* and *Tradition and an Individual Talent*, Heaney makes it clear that he has no desire to imitate the Scots poet Hugh MacDiarmid, for example, by following the nationalist writer's path into what he would regard as the blind-alley of obscure dialect poetry. Why should he feel obliged to do this anyway, since his people had taken the language of their conquerors and fashioned it into the material from which some of the greatest literature written in English had been composed? It is a measure of the extent to which the "split culture of Ulster" manifests itself in Heaney's own life that, in the same collection of verse, he can on the one hand advocate a resurgence of the Irish language in a poem like *A New Song* and then, on the other, use a quotation from James Joyce's novel **Ulysses** in *Traditions* to remind the people of Ireland that they should be proud of the way Irish artists had used English as a tool with which to shape their own cultural identity.

The structure of 'Wintering Out'

Ambiguous in its attitude towards language; unsure whether to finish that exploration of the Irish myth begun in **Door into the Dark** or to escape from it; unable to offer a way forward out of the Ulster crisis; its lack of a unifying vision recognized by the poet himself in his division of the book into two parts – **Wintering Out** should represent a low-point in Heaney's artistic career. Yet, paradoxically, it is in this third volume of verse that he finally breaks free from those critics who wished to label him as a "trout-tickling gypsy lad"[61] whose rather old-fashioned nature poetry was chiefly memorable for its instantly accessible "PQ, i.e. peasant quality".[62]

Wintering Out commands greater attention than either of the two earlier books, not only because it continues Yeats' epic attempt to give the Irish "a mythology that marries them to rock and hill"[63], but also because of the intense intellectual and imaginative demands it makes upon its readers. Many students who respond enthusiastically to the vivid depiction of childhood and rural life in **Death of a Naturalist** and then start to falter when Heaney invites them to follow him into the dark of his second volume, are bewildered by the thematic complexity of **Wintering Out**, encompassing as it does myth, legend, history, geography, linguistics, marriage and family life. No longer can it be said that Heaney is speaking simply, for and to simple people. Like T.S. Eliot before him – or his admired English contemporary, Geoffrey Hill – Heaney now demands from his audience a highly educated sense of history and literature. For example, he expects them to know who Edmund Spenser was, or the Tollund Man, or the Mummers of Lough Erne. They must be able to appreciate the significance of unattributed quotations from a **Veue of the Present State of Ireland** in *Bog Oak*, and Shakespeare's **Henry V** or Joyce's **Ulysses** in *Traditions*. Again, Heaney expects his audience to understand, without having it explained to them in the poem, why figures like Spenser or "the wandering Bloom" mean so much to him.

The reader of **Wintering Out** requires not only a high degree of cultural awareness, but also a powerful and flexible imagination. Preoccupied with the enduring qualities of myth, with the idea that history occurs in cycles, and with the concept of poetry as dream or trance, the poems of Heaney's third volume ignore the constraints of a conventional time-scale. In works like *Bog Oak, Servant Boy, The Last Mummer* or *The Tollund Man*, for example, the reader is led in and out of the worlds of legend, prehistory, the recorded past, the present and the future as though through some surreal maze. *The Last Mummer* and *The Tollund Man* present this movement through time in three carefully structured sections: the first is set in the present day; the second takes an over-view, placing its subject in an historical perspective; the third section progresses beyond the temporal sphere, moving into dream-vision in the case of *The Last Mummer* or projection of the future in *The Tollund Man*.

The stronger the atmosphere of trance or seance, the more volatile Heaney's distortion of time becomes. On the second line of the second verse in *Bog Oak*, he suddenly lifts that poem out of the solid, physical world onto a supernatural plane. From this point onwards, Heaney mediates powerfully between literal and symbolic, temporal and timeless. The "softening ruts" of that cart-track which he stands upon now, in the late twentieth-century, are at once an actual pathway and also that never-ending route towards self-destruction trodden by Irishmen throughout the centuries of religious strife. The "geniuses" who creep towards him represent, simultaneously, past, present and future victims of that conflict. The "smoke" and "mizzling rain" which obscure the poet's physical sight clear his mind's eye like a stimulant, enabling him to glimpse his vision of druidic and Elizabethan Ireland.

Heaney's unconventional treatment of time is part of a general movement away from the naturalism of his earlier verse which serves to compound the difficulty of **Wintering Out**. In **Death of a Naturalist** and many of the poems from **Door into the Dark**, the poet's chief concern was to recreate, as precisely and as sensuously as possible, the experiences of childhood and rural life. In this third volume, the earlier, exuberant delight in imagery is replaced by a diction as bleak and austere as the theme of the book itself. The lush details so characteristic of earlier poems like *Churning Day* or *Thatcher* are replaced by thumb-nail sketches as rare in this wintry landscape as that "straggle of fodder/stiffened on snow" in *Servant Boy* – "A nimble snout of flood/licks over stepping stones" in *Gifts of Rain*; a "Brigid's Cross" lies "yellowing in some outhouse" in *Traditions*.

Sound-effects, too, are used subtly and sparingly, without that intense matching of sound and meaning found in poems like *Death of a Naturalist* or *Beyond Sargasso*. The alliterated letter "b" on the second line of *Servant Boy*, for example, offers a momentary release of anger in a poem that is otherwise distanced and contemplative. The sense of menace and mystery achieved in Part One of *The Last Mummer* is powerfully realised because Heaney relies upon assonance to achieve the effect for him, instead of overloading those appropriately stark and isolated couplets with alliteration and onomatopoeia.

Wintering Out also lacks the conventional narrative structure found in **Death of a Naturalist**. In his earlier work, Heaney seems concerned to explain and describe everything, leaving almost nothing to the imagination; but here the reverse is true. Instead of following a logical sequential pattern, the poems offer a series of puzzling, fragmented images in which the literal, the symbolic, the surreal and the mystical flow into each other. In *Gifts of Rain*, for example, that physically solid figure of the "Still mammal" fording the flood is transformed without warning into a symbolic representation of the poet himself, as the word "sounding" is made plural and at once changes identity dramatically by taking on its linguistic rather than its nautical meaning. Similarly, in Part Three, the precisely evoked River Moyola suddenly becomes a place of supernatural power, where the poet might hear "Soft voices of the dead ... whispering by the shore". Who "the dead" might be, Heaney does not say; and **Wintering Out** is full of unanswered questions: why did the mother in *Limbo* drown her baby? What are the circumstances behind the story of *Bye-Child*? Who are the people in *Good-Night*? The poet offers no answers. On the contrary, he compounds the book's sense of uneasy enquiry by presenting himself as just another uncertain, anxious questioner in poems like *The Other Side*, *Stump*, *Tinder* and *Wedding Day*.

The verse structure of **Wintering Out** suits the tone of the book perfectly. Those experiments in stress and shape pattern in work like *Beyond Sargasso* and *Bogland* are developed here so that in this volume, more than ever, the poem's appearance upon the page matches the act of tunnelling which it describes. The terse, concentrated lines of **Wintering Out** seem particularly appropriate to the cold, barren and violent landscape portrayed in the book. If poems about love and nature are out of place in the Ulster of the early 'seventies, so too are long, richly decorated lines of verse. The poems of **Wintering Out** have a gaunt, skeletal look to them. Disjointed in structure, they lie upon the page like splinters of experience which the reader must reassemble – just as somehow he must reassemble the fragment of Ulster society.

The reason why **Wintering Out** differs dramatically in diction, structure and narrative form from so much of Heaney's earlier work, is because in this third volume he attempts to unite what he has described as the "masculine" with the "feminine" mode of poetry. Many of the poems in **Death of a Naturalist** and **Door into the Dark** represent the "feminine" aspect of his art, in that they are works of "divination and revelation" in which *les vers* is *donnée*. Now, however, he introduces *les vers calculés* of "the masculine mode" in which "the language functions as a form of address, of assertion or command, and the poetic effort has to do with conscious quelling and control of the materials". In other words, instead of using poetry passively, to "set the darkness echoing" by evoking lost emotions, landscapes and experiences, he now wants to set it to work as an active force also, capable of conveying ideas and tackling intellectual problems.

Cerebral poetry of this type has no use for decorative imagery or diction, for such devices simply distract it from its purpose. "Masculine" verse employs the techniques of poetry, not to "release a flow" as a poet like Keats might have done, but in the manner of Gerard Manley Hopkins – as "a stimulant to the mind".[64] Words become important, not so much for the sound and rhythm they make or the *frisson* they provoke, but for the ideas they convey. Thus, when in **Wintering Out** Heaney uses imagery, he does so as the poet Coleridge might have done in works like *The Eolian Harp* or *This Lime-Tree Bower My Prison*: as a starting-point and stimulus for intellectual debate. In *Gifts of Rain*, for example, a depiction of the rain-swollen Moyola prepares the way for his statement about the relationship between "locale" and "utterance". In *The Tollund Man*, that scrupulously exact description of the photograph from Glob's book forms an introduction for the radical response to the Ulster violence in Part Two of the poem. Elsewhere, descriptive writing is used, not to create atmosphere as in *Death of a Naturalist*, but as a means by which a profound philosophical idea can be conveyed vividly and concisely. Heaney's complex views about the need of the Irish people to reach back beyond Christianity to their mythic roots, is captured in that metaphor from the end of *The Last Mummer* which marries Catholic and pagan belief in one startling image: "The moon's host elevated/in a monstrance of holly trees".

Summary and conclusion

Wintering Out must be studied in the context of the contemporary political situation in Ulster. Try as Heaney might in his third collection of verse to break fresh poetic ground by exploring developments in his personal life such as marriage, fatherhood and foreign travel, he was drawn back inexorably to the problems of his homeland. The "shared calling of blood" which bound him to the Catholic cause was partly responsible for this; yet by bidding for the Yeatsian role of national poet in **Door into the Dark**, Heaney had really brought the obligation of speaking out about Ulster upon himself. Divided in his loyalties, unwilling to reduce his art to the level of some "diagram of political attitudes", unable to find that practical solution to the crisis which has eluded the professional politicians, much of what Heaney has to say in **Wintering Out** is comfortless, offering the merest "notion" of survival.

And yet, paradoxically, the book is exciting, challenging, innovatory. Events in Ulster between 1969 and 1972 seemed to confirm the vision which Heaney had begun to explore in **Door into the Dark**, and gave him the confidence and incentive to search even more urgently for an "answering Irish myth" that could offer his people "emblems of adversity" through which they might understand and perhaps control the destructive forces at work in their society.

The "magical world-view" revealed by Heaney's explorations, as by those of Yeats before him, offers such a radical challenge to the all-powerful "agnostic world of economic interest" that it bewilders many of those readers who had responded so positively to the simple vision of **Death of a Naturalist**. Equally challenging was the poet's grafting of a new, tough, austere, so-called "masculine" mode of public address onto his earlier, more intimate and inspirational "feminine" verse, in order that he might achieve a poetic style evocative enough to express the "magical world-view" and at the same time intellectual enough to grapple with those ideas about language, myth and cultural identity for which the magic provides a unifying metaphor.

Wintering Out is a demanding, complex book, exhilerating in the range of its themes, radical in its vision and adventurous in its experimentation. If the poems demand more from the reader than those of **Death of a Naturalist**, that is because Heaney has moved out of the league of comfortably accessible nature poets towards something greater. In so far as events in Ulster accelerated this progression and encouraged him to adopt a sharper and yet more subtle poetic style with which to undertake his obligations as tribal poet, then – to borrow and redirect Ciaran Carson's ironic comment about **North** – Heaney's third volume is, indeed, an exhibition of the good that can come out of troubled times.

Notes and References

1. Alan Dures, **Modern Ireland**, London and New York: 1973, p. 78.
2. Heaney, *Old Derry's Walls*, **The Listener**, 24 October 1968, p. 522.
3. Dures, **Modern Ireland**, p. 100.
4. Ibid., p. 105.
5. Lord Windlesham, **Guardian**, 5 December 1972.
6. Heaney, *Out of London: Ulster's Troubles*, **New Statesman**, 1 July 1966, p. 23.
7. Heaney, *Old Derry's Walls*, pp. 522, 523, 522.
8. *Feeling into Words*, p. 56.
9. Heaney, *Views*, **The Listener**, 31 December 1970, p. 903.
10. *Belfast*, p. 30.
11. Heaney, *Mother Ireland*, **The Listener**, 7 December 1972, p. 790.
12. Heaney, *Lost Ulstermen*, **The Listener**, 26 April 1973, p. 550.
13. *Mossbawn*, p. 22.
14. *Belfast*, pp. 34, 37.
15. *Feeling into Words*, p. 44.
16. See Heaney's essay, *Englands of the Mind*, **Preoccupations**, pp. 150–169.
17. *Belfast*, p. 35.
18. **North**, p. 64.
19. *Belfast*, p. 35.
20. *The Sense of Place*, pp. 132, 136.
21. *Belfast*, p. 30.
22. **North**, p. 63.
23. *Belfast*, p. 34.
24. Ibid., pp. 34, 30, 34, 30.
25. Ibid., p. 34.
26. *Faith, Hope and Poetry*, p. 219.
27. W.H. Auden, *In Memory of W.B. Yeats*.
28. Ciaran Carson, *Escaped from the Massacre?*, **The Honest Ulsterman**, 50 Winter 1975, p. 186.
29. Heaney, *Mother Ireland*, p. 790.
30. Heaney, *Views*, p. 903.
31. *Belfast*, p. 32.
32. Quoted in James Sutherland (ed.), **The Oxford Book of Literary Anecdotes**, Oxford: 1975, p. 10.
33. Quoted on the cover of **Wintering Out**, Faber: 1972.
34. See for example Lowell's poem *A Quaker Graveyard in Nantucket*.
35. Heaney, *Views*, p. 903.

36 *Belfast*, pp. 33, 34.
37 Ibid., p. 33.
38 *Feeling into Words*, pp. 47, 56–7.
39 *The Fire i' the Flint*, p. 88.
40 *Feeling into Words*, p. 57.
41 Ibid., p. 57.
42 Idem.
43 Heaney, *Summoning Lazarus*, **The Listener**, 6 June 1974, p. 741.
44 *Feeling into Words*, pp. 57, 59, 57–8, 57.
45 Ibid., p. 57.
46 *The Sense of Place*, p. 135.
47 *Yeats as an Example?* p. 104.
48 *Feeling into Words*, p. 57.
49 *Yeats as an Example?*, p. 104.
50 Heaney, *Seamus Heaney Praises Lough Erne*, **The Listener**, 4 February 1971, p. 143.
51 *Yeats as an Example?*, p. 104.
52 James Randall, *An Interview with Seamus Heaney*, **Ploughshares**, 5,3, 1979, p. 20.
53 *The Sense of Place*, p. 135.
54 Ibid., p. 132.
55 *Belfast*, pp. 35, 36.
56 Ibid., p. 36.
57 *The Sense of Place*, p. 132.
58 *Lost Ulstermen*, p. 550.
59 *The Sense of Place*, p. 131.
60 *Belfast*, p. 35.
61 Edward Pygge, **The Review**, 22 June 1970, p. 62.
62 *Celtic Fringe, Viking Fringe*, p. 255.
63 Quoted in *Yeats as an Example?*, p. 105.
64 *The Fire i' the Flint*, pp. 88, 85.

Chapter Four

'North'

The divided structure of 'North'

North was published in June 1975, three years after Seamus Heaney had abandoned Ulster for life in the South of Ireland. Like **Wintering Out**, this final collection of verse represented in the **Selected Poems**[1] is divided into two parts, as though to signify the poet's continual obsession with and ambiguous response to the history and politics of Ireland. Contemporary events in Ulster haunt Part One of **Wintering Out** with the sense of menace and disquiet of an indefinable bad dream from which the poet tries unsuccessfully to escape in Part Two[2]; but in **North**, both sections confront the "urgency"[3] of the political and social crisis head-on, and the two-part structure of the collection represents, not the conflicting impulses of commitment and disengagement, but an attempt to cope with the twin pressures of offering a contemplative and an immediate response to the situation.

To the readers of Heaney's *Belfast* essay, Part Two of **North** would come as a shock, for here the writer who once declared that "I have always listened for poems," breaks his vow not "to start squaring up to contemporary events with more will than ways to deal with them." Contemporary events dominate this section of the book, providing the titles for poems three and four of the *Singing School* sequence, or intruding upon the final section of *Whatever You Say Say Nothing* in the form of a "new camp for the internees" and the latest slogan "chalked up" on a wall in the Ballymurphy Estate of Belfast. Contemporary figures like the political commentator Cruise O'Brien – even the Catholic Scottish football team, "Celtic" – are mentioned. The poetic voice used here by Heaney resorts to cliche, colloquialism, media jargon and swearing, in order to achieve a kind of "street-wise" immediacy which, with its unsubtle structures of decasyllabic rhyming couplets and quatrains, or hurried, epistolary verse paragraphs, looks and sounds totally alien to the densely-worked, "tunnelling" verse forms established in **Wintering Out**.

Gone, too, from this section of **North** is that former belief in the need to strike a balance between "humane reason" and "the religious intensity of the violence" to which Heaney subscribed in his 1974 essay, *Feeling into Words*. Losing patience with the "liberal papist note" and "those sanctioned, old, elaborate retorts" which deplore the violence but do nothing to understand or resolve it, he seeks instead to emulate the immediate gut response of an artist like Goya who, as Heaney puts it, "flourished/The stained cape of his heart as history charged". The opening lines of *Whatever You Say Say Nothing*, the poem which deals most directly with the Ulster crisis, sum up this new mood of emotional, unpremeditated engagement:

> I'm writing just after an encounter
> With an English journalist in search of "views
> on the Irish thing".

In works like this, Heaney surrenders unequivocally to the "shared calling of blood" and makes statements which are clearly hostile to the Protestant cause. *Orange Drums, Tyrone, 1966*, for example, describes those instruments as "giant tumours" upon the bodies of the marchers, and "Summer 1969" opens with a bitterly partisan response to the Belfast riots in August of that year:

> While the Constabulary covered the mob
> Firing into the Falls, I was suffering
> Only the bullying sun of Madrid.[4]

When Heaney came to choose the **Selected Poems**, he included only four from what he has called the "explicit" second section of **North**, compared with eleven from the "symbolic"[5] first. Amongst the excluded poems are those which make the most politically committed, emotional and immediate response to the Ulster crisis. The absence of these five pieces means that if a reader's only experience of **North** comes from the **Selected Poems**, he will receive a distorted impression of that volume's structure and intention. The fact that Heaney was later prepared to sacrifice the structural integrity of **North** in this way suggests that, with the benefit of five years hindsight, he now regarded the decision to "wrench the rhythms" of his "writing procedure" as a mistake.

Heaney's response to the pressures of the Ulster crisis

The question remains: what was it about the poet's attitude to events in Ireland in the early 'seventies which caused him to break so dramatically from his carefully fostered artistic principles? The causes of this *volte-face* were increased feelings of guilt and of exasperation.

Part of the problem was Heaney's move from Belfast to Glanmore, County Wicklow, in the summer of 1972. To some observers, this act smacked of betrayal. Indeed, Heaney had unwittingly laid himself open to such criticism in an ironically prophetic essay of July 1966 where, commenting on the probable impact of the gathering crisis upon the artistic community of Ulster, he remarks that "the uncommitted and the sceptical tend to leave".[6] Eight years later, the pressure placed upon Heaney to prove that his flight south signified neither scepticism nor lack of commitment, was compounded by his growing awareness of the fact that now more than ever people were looking to him, as one of Ulster's most famous artists, to "'say' something about 'the situation'".[7]

If there was little of comfort that Heaney could offer on this subject in **Wintering Out**, he had even less to say now. The three years which had elapsed since the publication of his third book had brought an intensification of sectarian division and an increase in the violence which accompanied it. Perhaps more depressing still, the one positive development during this period – the establishment of a power-sharing executive which offered some say in government to the Catholic minority – was destroyed in 1974 when Protestant workers, fearing that a proposed "Council of Ireland" was the first move towards absorption into the Republic, mobilised themselves as the "Ulster Workers' Council" and staged a general strike which brought down the executive and re-established the old political and social dead-lock.

Written against such a background, even those five supposedly "explicit" poems, in which Heaney might be expected to say something recklessly dramatic simply to break out of the impasse, offer no radically partisan solutions. Examples of fighting-talk about Orange "greed" and "open minds as open as a trap" are far outweighted by the overwhelming sense of impotent despair which pervades Part Two of **North**. Even as he wrenches "the rhythms" of his "writing procedure" to accommodate their demands, Heaney turns bitterly on the people represented by that "English journalist" in *Whatever You Say Say Nothing* for demanding his "'views/On the Irish thing'". What could he possibly say to them? As early as 1972, the suggestion that the people of Ulster were "wintering out/the back-end of a bad year" seemed a barely acceptable response to the crisis; now, after three further years of mounting violence and unrest which had placed the poet himself "back in winter/Quarters", such an answer appeared totally discredited. Nor could anything be achieved by using his verse to report the situation: the hotels of Belfast were already packed with "media-men" who, despite all their "zoom lenses, recorders and coiled leads", were incapable of prompting a successful political initiative from Britain. Ulster might be suffering worse than ever; yet, by 1975, those sufferings were compounded by the bitter realisation that, in Heaney's words, "bad news" was "no longer news".[8]

From public to private response: the changed role of the poet in 'North'

In the light of such knowledge, the only valid response which Heaney feels able to offer, even in those "explicit" poems from the second part of **North**, is to trust his own feelings – to look in upon himself in order to analyse and record the effect which the crisis has had upon him as both citizen and artist. As he observed at the time of the book's publication: "poets from Northern Ireland ... will only be worth listening to if they are saying something about and to themselves."[9] Thus the poems of Part Two explore the range of Heaney's reactions, from the impotent rage of the "Unacknowledged Legislator" who can only dream of how he might "move the world", to the self-disgust of the "fork-tongued" "liberal papist" – one who will "tremble near the flames" of violent change, but wants "no truck/With the actual firing" – and lastly, to the guilt and despair of the poet who, "for all this art and sedentary trade" is "incapable" of finding answers, preferring to look at Goya's paintings of brutal oppression rather than stand on the Falls Road "where the real thing still happened".[10]

Those "explicit" works from **North** which did achieve inclusion in the **Selected Poems** might be less outspoken or immediate than the ones Heaney left out, but they reveal the same pessimistic shifting of emphasis from a didactic to a personal response. Here, too, the poet despairs of finding solutions or educating his audience through his explorations of the Ulster crisis, concentrating again on its effect upon himself. In *A Constable Calls*, for example, he could have used the policeman's visit as a means of offering some general insight into the "siege mentality" of the Catholic population as a whole. By describing the event from a child's point of view, rather than looking at it with the benefit of adult hindsight or even through the eyes of his father, Heaney reduces the perspective of the poem so that, for all its references to "the boot of the law", it reads more as a study of childhood guilt than as a political statement.

This same note is struck with even greater emphasis in *The Ministry of Fear*, where the dedication of the poem to Seamus Deane, the relaxed, colloquial verse paragraphs and the use of "you" as the term of address, all create the impression that the reader is intruding upon the private correspondence of two old friends. Once again, the idea that the Catholic population is "Besieged within the siege"[11] by a culturally and politically dominant enemy tribe is conveyed in purely personal terms as Heaney recalls how the police stopped and searched his car one night, shining their torches on Deane's

"'Svelte dictions'". Once again, the opportunity to relate the poet's experience to that of his people as a whole is declined.

Act of Union takes this personalizing of public events to its extreme. Here, Heaney attempts to heal the breach created in **Wintering Out** between his love poetry and his poems about Ulster, by describing the political "Act of Union" which brought Ireland under English control in terms of the sexual act of union between man and woman. In this poem, as in so much of Part Two of **North**, that sense of obligation to "'say' something about 'the situation'" seems to have wrenched the "rhythms" of his "writing procedures"; double-meaning is piled remorselessly upon double-meaning until, in an effort to equate the growing foetus with Ulster Unionism, the conceit collapses under the strain: "The act sprouted an obstinate fifth column/Whose stance is growing unilateral." As with *A Constable Calls* and *The Ministry of Fear*, this poem leaves the reader thinking about what might have been said, rather than about what is said. Attempting to be both love poem and political statement, *Act of Union* achieves neither aim. Politically, the poem offers no insight into the Irish problem. It merely reiterates a number of truisms and well-worn opinions: the Unionists are "parasitical", "ignorant", and angry; the conflict has happened before; no "treaty" seems capable of achieving a solution. It is as a love poem, however, that *Act of Union* fails most conspicuously: to cast male and female in the roles of imperial power and exploited colony is to introduce an important feminist dimension to the work; but yet again, Heaney does not follow it through. "I am still imperially/Male," he tells the woman at the start of Part Two, "leaving you with the pain"; and in the same way he leaves the reader with a series of unanswered questions, preferring as before simply to describe the act of union and the personal feelings of disquiet and pessimism which it provokes in him.

The *Bog Poems* of 'North'

The "symbolic" poems from Part One of **North** also show the poet retreating from a public to a more private position. Nowhere is this more clearly seen than in the development of Heaney's response to P.V. Glob's book **The Bog People**. In 1972, he had found the work intellectually stimulating and challenging, for it seemed to offer him positive new insights into the condition of Ireland – insights which might aid his search for that "answering Irish myth". An interview given in the December of the same year indicates just how much **The Bog People** had helped Heaney to understand, and thus to control, the situation in Ulster:

> The Early Iron Age in Northern Europe is a period that offers very satisfactory imaginative parallels to the history of Ireland at the moment ... You have a society in the Iron Age where there was ritual blood-letting. You have a society where girls' heads were shaved for adultery, you have a religion centring on the territory, on a goddess of the ground and of the land, and associated with sacrifice. Now in many ways the fury of Irish Republicanism is associated with a religion like this, with a female goddess who has appeared in various guises. She appears as Cathleen ni Houlihan in Yeats' plays; she appears as Mother Ireland. I think that the Republican ethos is a feminine religion, in a way. It seems to me that there are satisfactory parallels between this religion and time and our own time.[12]

The positive influence of Glob's book can be seen in the poem *The Tollund Man*, where Heaney takes the dominant image from **The Bog People** and uses it to project his own radical solution to the problems of Ulster.

Three years later, the poet's attitude has completely changed. Instead of using the images from **The Bog People** as a point of departure in his exploration of the Irish situation, Heaney works more like a midwife, writing as though his task requires him to do no more than bring the poems to birth rather than shape them to any intellectual design. The midwife analogy is an apt one, for throughout the *Bog Poems* of **North**, the poet uses language associated with birth to describe the creation of these strange images: The "Bog Queen" rises from the dark when her "slimy birthcord/of bog" is cut; the Grauballe Man emerges out of the peat "bruised like a forceps baby"; the hair of the girl in *Punishment* is "unswaddled". These are the "children" delivered by Heaney's poetry – or, rather, casting him again in the role explored in such poems as *Gifts of Rain* – these are the spirits which come to the medium's call in a time of violence. Too pessimistic now to demand an answer from them as in *The Tollund Man*, Heaney simply presents the Irish people with their "befitting emblems of adversity", their images for the age. Fifty years earlier, Yeats had also watched "Things fall apart" and asked himself "what rough beast" – what new, post-Christian deity, "its hour come round at last",[13] – might replace the crucified Christ as a symbol for the times. In the *Bog Poems* from **North**, Heaney offers an answer to his predecessor's question.

The poet's increased pessimism about Ireland is reflected here not only in the fact that this sequence of poems is concerned more with the creation of images than with looking for answers, but also in the changed nature of the images themselves. In 1972, when it was still possible to speak of the crisis in terms of "wintering out/the back-end of a bad year", Heaney's description of the Tollund Man could portray his sacrifice as a positive act, and present him as something akin to Chaucer's "holy blisful martyr",[14] a religious figure endowed with healing powers.

By 1975, it is not the mild, sacrificial "Bridegroom to the goddess" but the rapacious goddess herself who provides the poet's "emblem". This new personification of "the fury of Irish Republicanism" is far more disturbing than those cold women portrayed in **Wintering Out**. Where the Tollund Man represented serenity and wholeness, the figures of 1975 are grotesquely mutilated. Heaney spares his readers no details, exploring with clinical thoroughness "the cavings/of stomach and socket" of the Bog Queen; the "slashed throat" of the Grauballe Man; that head like an "exhumed gourd" in *Punishment*. These haunting faces from Glob's book belong to victims of Iron Age sacrifices; but they might as easily be those of the inmates of a Nazi concentration camp – or of the "betraying sisters" from *Punishment*, tarred, feathered and chained to railings by their fellow Catholics in twentieth-century Ulster for fraternising with British soldiers. In the dreadful cycle of Irish history, images from two thousand years ago match all too successfully the headlines of today, "outstaring" – as Heaney writes at the end of *Strange Fruit* is an oblique reference to *The Tollund Man* – "What had begun to feel like reverence".

One of the reasons why the images portrayed in the *Bog Poems* from **North** are so powerful is because they suggest a sense of nightmare. Heaney achieves this surreal effect by totally confusing the reader's terms of reference. Not only does he shift the narrator's stance between empathy and detachment in the four poems, but his description of each of the figures creates an impression of dislocation by juxtaposing a sequence of jarringly antagonistic images: human against natural, beautiful against grotesque, small against vast. Thus, in three short lines and a mere eight words from *Bog Queen*, an historical figure is transformed into a mythical nature goddess by a conceit worthy of the "Metaphysical" poets:

> ... phoenician stitchwork
> retted on my breasts'
>
> soft moraines.

This sense of dislocation is even more intense in *The Grauballe Man* where the victim's "slashed throat" is at once a mark of hideous physical mutilation and yet, at the same time, something natural and beautiful – a gateway which opens "inwards to a dark/ elderberry place" beyond the historical world. "Who will say 'corpse'", Heaney writes in this poem, "to his vivid cast"? And indeed, the effect achieved by that metaphysical technique employed in the *Bog Poems* is to create a series of magically elusive figures who are constantly changing shape and identity under the poet's scrutiny: at one moment victims of some ancient ritual; at the next, deities of a natural religion themselves or emblems of the violence in Ulster.

Perhaps the most disturbing thing about these images is the poet's own response to them. Studying the *Bog Poems* from **North**, the reader gets the impression that Heaney's reluctance to shape these works to some positive purpose stems not only from his increased sense of political despair, but also from a paralysis of will. The poet seems to be so mesmerized by the power of the images he has created, that he can do no more than gaze at them repeatedly with morbid fascination – hence that large proportion of the poems given over to the unsettling, obsessive cataloguing of grim physical detail. Even more unnerving is the tone of voice used here. The note of reverential awe found in *The Tollund Man* is replaced by something much more intimate. *Bog Queen*, for example, is written in the first person; and in *Punishment*, Heaney speaks as though he too "can feel the tug/of the halter" around the neck of the "Little adulteress". "I almost love you", he tells her; and the dominant impression gained by the reader here, as in *The Ministry of Fear*, is of intruding upon something private – only in this case that something is the correspondence, not of friends, but of lovers.

This poetic sequence from **North** is the bleakest in the **Selected Poems**, because in these works Heaney reveals himself to be, like the poet John Keats, "half in love with easeful Death".[15] Fascinated by the images of destruction which his art has released, he seems to become more and more absorbed in his own life-denying trance while all around him "Things fall apart".

Paradoxically, it is this very self-absorption which breaks the spell. By turning inwards instead of outwards, Heaney inevitably releases those feelings of guilt and divided loyalty which form the essence of his poetic consciousness. The more he seeks escape by brooding upon the strange creations of his imagination, the more they rise up and force him to examine his conscience about Ulster. Thus, the image of the Grauballe Man brings ultimately neither oblivion nor healing. On the contrary, it is "hung in the scales" before Heaney as a symbol of judgement and retribution. This reawakening of the poet's sense of moral awareness does nothing to check the negative impulses of the poem. Rather, it enhances them. The sight of the Grauballe Man draws from Heaney a brutally frank declaration of his partisan sympathies which places him alongside those Catholics from *Whatever You Say Say Nothing* who, "in their deepest heart of hearts",[16] believe the violence inflicted upon their Protestant neighbours to be an act of divine vengeance. Heaney has to admit that the Catholic in him also sees a kind of "beauty" as well as "atrocity" in each "hooded victim" of the Ulster conflict. Even more frighteningly at odds with the "liberal Papist note" are the final stanzas of *Punishment*. Here again, the poet is driven from contemplation to confession when the sight of that "poor scapegoat" of the Iron Age forces him to confess that he would have done as little to save her life as he does for her twentieth-century "betraying sisters". The last two lines of this poem are the most chilling and dauntlessly honest in the **Selected Poems**. Here Heaney strips away the veneer of "civilized outrage" and surrenders to the darker, deeper forces of "tribal" vengeance. With the final statement of *Punishment*, the negative impulses released in the *Bog Poems* achieve fulfilment. If even the poet can abandon his declared fidelity to "the perspectives of a humane reason" and cast "the stones of silence" while a girl is tortured, what hope is left?

The use of symbolism for self-analysis

This use of symbolism as a means of self-analysis dominates the image-patterns of **North**. In *Viking Dublin: Trial Pieces*, for example, Heaney's description of the excavated remains found in the old Norse city is not used simply to provide the starting-point for another poem about the relationship between land and history, as would have been the case in *Bogland*. Instead, the "buoyant/migrant line" incised on the "trial piece" by that ancient, anonymous artist enters the poet's own "longhand", becoming a "worm of thought" which he follows "into the mud" of his confused mind. Heaney's sense of self-absorption is expressed even more clearly in *Exposure*. This poem is set on a remarkable winter's evening when "A comet that was lost/Should be visible at sunset"; yet the author, once renowned for the quality of his nature poetry, is no longer concerned to capture the scene with the lush sounds and images he might have employed in **Death of a Naturalist**. Rather than considering the comet or the Wicklow landscape on their own terms, Heaney uses them to signify and articulate the conflict within him. Thus, the rain which "comes down through the alders" becomes a metaphor for his divided self. The sound of it condemns his flight from Ulster, the sight of it recalls "The diamond absolutes" of art and affirms his dedication to the poet's calling. Even the "comet's pulsing rose" cannot break Heaney's introspection. It is absorbed into the scheme of his internal debate as a "once-in-a-lifetime portent" whose "million tons of light" do not bring a message of cosmic significance, but symbolise nothing more than one man's missed opportunities.

Hercules against Antaeus: The symbolic figures of 'North'

Just as Heaney uses the poetic landscape of **North** to analyse his own feelings, so he peoples that landscape with figures who do not offer solutions to the Irish crisis, but instead symbolize the various conflicting responses it has provoked in him. That sense of divided loyalty considered in the last chapter and expressed so forcefully in essays like *Belfast* and *Feeling into Words*, achieves poetic definition through these symbols. On the one hand, Heaney establishes the figure of "humane reason"; on the other, that darker, instinctual being who is capable of granting "the religious intensity of the violence its deplorable authenticity and complexity".[17]

The clash between these two irreconcilable aspects of the artist's personality is personified most vividly in *Hercules and Antaeus*. Here, Antaeus, son of the earth, a "mould-hugger" who renews his "black powers" by "feeding off the territory" and draws new strength from his mother whenever he touches the ground, signifies the tribal poet in Heaney, whose gut-response to the "shared calling of blood" sends him tunnelling for "antediluvian lore" with the patience and intuitive skill of the water-diviner. Hercules represents what Heaney would describe as the "masculine" aspect of his personality and art which regards "mastery and penetration" rather than the ability to "surrender to experience"[18] as the chief poetic virtues.

These two fundamental, antithetical symbols create deeper resonances. His "mind big with golden apples", and "his future hung with trophies", the figure of Hercules broadens to suggest ideas of conquest and historical destiny. As he "lifts and banks Antaeus", the child of the Earth-Mother, Hercules seems to merge into the "imperially/Male" persona from *Act of Union*. Once again, the process of colonization is reinterpreted as a struggle between individuals; only this time the parts are not played by male and female lovers but by the "masculine" and "feminine" elements of the artist's personality.

Explored further, the figure of Hercules, hero of Graeco-Roman mythology, slayer of monsters and enemy of chaos, represents not only reason, masculinity and imperialism, but yet another facet of Heaney's complex response to Ireland – his desire "To lure the tribal shoals to epigram/And order"[19] through his poetry. The figure of Hercules, however, is too much the man of action, too self-confident, to represent accurately the poet's bewildered, hesitant response to the contemporary situation in Ulster. A more satisfactory symbol emerges in poems like *Strange Fruit*, *Kinship* and *Exposure*, where Heaney refines the image of Hercules by removing the active element and replacing it with something more "bookish", while at the same time emphasising the connotations of reason, order, masculinity and imperialism. Out of Hercules is born the compromised, parasitical figure of the Graeco-Roman scholar: a man who flourishes on the peace and security provided by the ruthless exercise of imperial power, but turns a blind eye to its cruelties. In the *Mother Ireland* interview published in December 1972, Heaney shows contempt for this figure when, having described the historic parallels between Early Iron Age blood-sacrifice and the "fury of Irish Republicanism", he remarks:

> They are observed with amazement and a kind of civilized tut-tut by Tacitus in the first century A.D. and by leader-writers in the **Daily Telegraph** in the 20th century.[20]

Viewed in the light of this comment, the symbol of the Graeco-Roman scholar in **North** becomes a yard-stick by which Heaney measures his own response to "the fury of Irish Republicanism", and also provides him with yet another focus for self-criticism. In *Strange Fruit*, for example, his own fascination with the *Bog People* and all that their images represent, is conveyed in a reference to Diodorus Siculus, a Greek scholar of the first century B.C. who, like Heaney, was concerned with history and, like Heaney again, "confessed" – the choice of word is significant – "His gradual ease" among "the likes" of that "terrible/Beheaded girl" who so enthralls his twentieth-century counterpart. In Part VI of *Kinship*, the image of the classical scholar is put to more desperate use. The "Antaeus" in Heaney rounds upon its opposite number in the guise of that Roman historian criticised in *Mother Ireland* and, by describing what is happening to Ulster as bitterly and brutally as possible, tries to shock him into some kind of positive response. The cruel, almost ghoulish way in which the poet is now seeking to establish his "grove" of inspiration, not in the natural world, but on "an old crannog/piled by the fearful dead"; his terrifyingly callous description of how the Irish slaughter "for the common good" while "the goddess swallows/our love and terror" – all possess the urgency of a cry for help. It is as though that side of Heaney's nature which is drawn by the "shared calling of blood" into a fascinated contemplation of violence, is trying to goad his humane, rationalist self into doing something to snap him out of that life-denying trance before it is too late. The scholar, however, does nothing. The final poem from *North* reveals him to be as compromised and uncertain as ever, as he sits "weighing and weighing" his "responsible *tristia*".

The image of Antaeus is also explored throughout the book; but like that of Hercules, it serves to articulate the poet's sense of dilemma rather than to offer a way forward. If the symbol of the classical scholar exposes the failure of "humane reason", the development of the Antaeus figure prevents Heaney from swerving to the opposite extreme. The part played in this process by the images described in works like *The Grauballe Man*, *Punishment* and *Kinship* has already been discussed; but even in *Hercules and Antaeus* itself, Heaney turns upon the source of the darker side of his poetic imagination and condemns it as "a dream of loss", dismissing its narcotic hold upon him as "pap for the dispossessed".

Like his exploration of the symbol of the classical scholar, Heaney's examination of the Antaeus figure culminates in the final poem of **North**; and again, the image is ambiguous. By describing himself as a "wood-kerne", the poet appears to side in the colonial war with those "geniuses" from *Bogland* seen creeping out of "woodes and glennes" by Edmund Spencer; for the "rough rug-headed kerns" /sic/ were the native soldiers of Ireland whom that earlier representative of English imperialism, Shakespeare's Richard II, sought to "supplant" in his "Irish wars".[21] Yet this particular "kerne" has "Escaped from the massacre", or, to put it less kindly, fled the field of battle. Moreover, his main aim seems to be to imitate *The Last Mummer* and the figure from Part I of *Gifts of Rain*: more concerned with survival than resistance, he takes "protective colouring/From bole and bark, feeling/Every wind that blows".

Ultimately, the "Sky-born" proves as helpless as the "mould-hugger". Nothing demonstrates more graphically Heaney's sense of impasse in his response to the Irish situation than those final images from *Hercules and Antaeus* where the two champions are left in a state of deadlock. Held in the air, Antaeus is powerless; but the "remorseless V" which keeps him prisoner keeps Hercules immobile as well. The complexities of the contemporary political situation force the poet to sit "weighing and weighing" his response. In such a world, there seems no place for the unambiguous gesture, the heroic act. Antaeus, having "bequeathed" his heritage to "elegists" rather than men of action, becomes a "sleeping giant", just as Gaelic Balor, English Byrthnoth, the American Indian Sitting Bull – heroes of every race that has ever faced the threat of conquest – must perish in the modern age.

The poet as Hamlet

It is appropriate that when Heaney makes a direct rather than inferred identification of himself with a symbolic figure, he chooses "Hamlet the Dane". The image neatly expresses his sense of divided loyalty and the preoccupations of his art. More than this, the reference to **Hamlet** provides a key to the interpretation of **North**. As in Shakespeare's play, so here: much of the tension of the work comes from watching a deeply sensitive and cultured intelligence – imbued on the one hand with a sharply ironic self-awareness and on the other a powerful sense of obligation – wrestle with a profound moral dilemma.

To place so much responsibility for the book's success on the effectiveness of this personal theme is to tread dangerous ground. First – and this is partly why **North** received such an unenthusiastic response from Ulster reviewers[22] – it invites the charge of self-indulgence. Why should the anguished soul-searching of one man who has, on his own admission, "Escaped from the massacre", deserve so much attention when so many other Irish people less fortunate than himself are suffering physical hardships as a result of the violence? That trying-out of images might represent an attempt at self-analysis; but it can just as easily be taken for role-playing or a sign of the re-emergence of "big-eyed Narcissus" from *Personal Helicon*. Heaney's description of himself as a "wood-kerne" may create effective historical and political resonances; but the additional comment that he has "grown long-haired/And thoughtful" while his companions have perished in "the massacre" is distastefully smug and self-regarding.

Sometimes – as that somewhat pretentious portrait by Edward McGuire on the back cover of the first edition suggests – Heaney seems to be posturing in **North**, striking a false note. How can he deride his poetry as "responsible *tristia*" or accuse himself of "blathering" – and then take the trouble to publish his work? Those tormented questions on the purpose of art in *Exposure* call to mind the complaints of the rock musician who makes his living by selling albums about the anguish of being a "star". Indeed, Heaney goes some way towards acknowledging the charge that he is trading off the Ulster crisis when, in *Punishment*, he confesses himself to be "the artful voyeur" of suffering.

The most significant example of posturing, however, is Heaney's identification of himself with Hamlet, for it suggests that the poet's contemplation of his dilemma in **North** deserves the same attention and respect as Shakespeare's masterpiece. The two have less in common than at first appears. Shakespeare uses Hamlet's personal predicament to conduct a profound philosophical study of fundamental human themes. Heaney, on the other hand, having moved away from the more intellectual, so-called "masculine" poetic mode of **Wintering Out**, and retreated in upon himself, does not exploit his response to the Ulster crisis for this purpose. For him, it is enough to describe the emotional impact that political events have on one man. Instead of soliloquies about life and death, he offers evocations of guilt, fear, remorse, exasperation.

The public poems of 'North': Heaney's exploration of the "Irish myth" resumed and concluded

Just how far Heaney's introspection weakens or enhances **North** must be, ultimately, a matter of personal judgement. Where some see self-indulgence and self-inflation, others are absorbed by the poet's efforts to come to terms with his own feelings and find, in his reaction to the situation in Ulster, a model for their own response to moral pressure.

It would be false to give the impression that **North** is entirely concerned with Heaney's retreat into himself. In several of the poems he does resume the role of tribal poet pursued so vigorously in **Wintering Out**. The obvious examples of this are the *Bog Poems*, where Heaney offers his people more "befitting emblems of adversity"; but in most of *Viking Dublin: Trial Pieces* and all of *North*, he does not merely evoke or respond to the "emblem" but, as in the case of *The Tollund Man*, shapes it intellectually, so that it bears a message for the whole tribe. It is in poems like these, where – to use the poet's own words about Hopkins – the "masculine" and "feminine" poetic modes, the "doctrine" and the "description" achieve "intense communion",[23] that Heaney's work comes closest to greatness.

The positive, shaping spirit of *Viking Dublin* and *North* is suggested by the poet's description of himself in these two poems as someone who is searching for answers again, not by examining his own soul, but by looking outward into the world beyond. Thus, at the start of *North*, he returns to a "long strand" on the northern coast of Ireland and stares out across the Atlantic Ocean towards Iceland and Greenland. In *Viking Dublin*, he resumes that questioning of the dead begun in *Gifts of Rain* and *Bog Oak*. The final stanza of the poem subdues the hesitations expressed in Part IV and presents the poet as a figure of authority, courage and determination. Instead of retreating in horror from "the skull-capped ground" of Dublin, he strides towards it boldly, like a hunter closing on his prey.

Heaney's questions find answers in both poems, providing him with startling new "emblems of adversity" to place beside those of the *Bog People*. By introducing the image of the Vikings into his work, the poet brings to his already sombre vision of the "Irish myth" an element darker than anything he has ever used before. In a manner reminiscent, yet again, of Yeats' *The Second Coming*, Heaney offers his people a frightening new emblem totally different from the stoical servant boy or even the haunting figure of the Bog Queen. For an age of horrific murder he provides the image of a ruthless murderer, one who, with "a butcher's aplomb", could "spread out your lungs"; one to whom "peace" meant a breathing-space in which to prepare for the next round of killings. In Part V of *Viking Dublin* as before in Part II of *The Tollund Man*, Heaney risks "blasphemy" by making a bold and, to Christian eyes, shocking gesture: instead of recoiling in "civilized outrage" from the dark, pagan force he has invoked, he embraces it. "Old fathers", he cries in a phrase which seems to parody the language of "the Marian litany",[24] "be with us." The implications of this prayer are grim: if ever-intensifying violence is to be the fate of Ireland, then fierce Viking cunning and toughness will be needed to survive it.

As in earlier poems like *The Last Mummer* and *Gifts of Rain*, Heaney uses these emblems established by his "feminine" poetic mode as a starting-point for the intellectual speculation associated with his "masculine" voice. In the two works from **North**, the transition from "feminine" image to "masculine" thought occurs with a new fluency and urgency; for unlike those silent figures from the bog, or the scarcely audible "voices of the dead ... whispering by the shore" of the River Moyola, the Vikings force their way into the analytical sections of the poem. In *North* itself, their "ocean-deafened voices" rise in "warning" from the "thundering" Atlantic waves; while in Part IV of *Viking Dublin*, the "trial piece" which had seemed to be nothing more than a museum curiousity comes suddenly and magically to life when, as though sending out an electrical charge, it transfers the spark of artistic inspiration from the "buoyant/migrant line" of its long-dead creator into the "longhand" of the living poet.

The message which the Vikings deliver so urgently to the Irish people here calls upon them to reconsider the geographical and historical implications of the term "North", to realise that if they are to understand what is happening in Ulster today, they must take into account the part which Scandinavian peoples have played in the history of Ireland. Just how important their role was, Heaney demonstrates in Part III of *Viking Dublin*. Taking up again the idea of a connection between "locale" and "utterance" explored in **Wintering Out**, he reminds his readers that the name of Ireland's major city is "spined and plosive" as the "clinker-built hull" of a Viking longship. As the early 'seventies archaeological excavations of the old Norse city which inspired this poem made clear, Dublin is built, literally and metaphorically, upon Scandinavian foundations. If "King Billy" and the Pope are integral elements of Ireland's folk-consciousness, then so are the Vikings – even in the confused and uneducated mind of "Jimmy Farrell", their presence assumes a fairy-tale significance.

The new insight into the "Irish myth", which Heaney offers here, is as radical, challenging and incomprehensible to the "agnostic world of economic interest" as that presented in *The Tollund Man*. Once again, the poet dares his people to break free from the stranglehold which Christianity exerts upon their sense of reality, to look deeper and more boldly into the history of Ireland. What *North* and *Viking Dublin* will help them to see there is the startling fact that the supposedly all-important sectarian divisions of Ulster are, ultimately, irrelevant to the real problem. The Vikings, who were playing the colonial game long before the English arrived, did not need to call each other "Catholic" or "Protestant" as an excuse for "hatreds and behindbacks". What conclusion can the poet draw from this except to say, despairingly, as he does in *Kinship*, that Ireland is a country "where nothing will suffice"? The land seems to be cursed, and the people fated to fight each other throughout history.

If the violence cannot be stopped, it can at least be mourned. This elegiac note, contrasting so dramatically with the other moods expressed in **North**, emerges in the *Bog Poems* where, in an image powerfully reminiscent of Michelangelo's *Pieta*. Heaney gazes lovingly at the martyred bodies of Grauballe Man or "Little adulteress". It achieves its most powerful expression, however, in *Funeral Rites*, when the poet unites the "Viking" and "Iron-Age" elements of the "Irish myth" to offer one final message to his tribe. This time, Heaney does not try to suggest ways of understanding, controlling or enduring the violence of Ulster –*North* and *Viking Dublin* have shown that to be impossible. Instead, he accepts "neighbourly murder" as a fact of Irish life and, as in *The Tollund Man*, tries to transform that evil miraculously into good. But whereas in *The Tollund Man* Heaney felt able to give the killings some meaning by regarding them as sacrifices from whose spilt blood peace might "germinate", the far bleaker circumstances of mid-seventies Ulster will not allow him even this degree of relief in *Funeral Rites*. All he can urge now is the thought that if, somehow, Catholic and Protestant could simply unite in their common grief, could bury and mourn their dead together, then perhaps, "the cud of memory" might be "allayed for once" and "arbitration/of the feud placated".

Once again, the message to the tribe is couched in the language, not of "agnostic ... economic interest" but of the "magical world-view", and demands a boldly imaginative response that few have the courage to make. Since no form of Christian ceremony would satisfy both Catholic and Protestants, the people must abandon church or chapel and, carrying their dead through the "megalithic doorway" to "the great chambers of Boyne", deliver them to the care of a deity far older than Christ. "Come fly with me," Heaney had urged his people in Part V of *Viking Dublin*, "come sniff the wind/with the expertise of the Vikings". If "those fabulous raiders" were killers, they were also daring adventurers; and it is only by emulating them, by having the nerve to risk everything in some desperate, liberating gesture of the kind described in *Funeral Rites*, that the citizens of Ireland can hope to break through the centuries-old hatred and achieve reconciliation.

The final section of this poem makes it the most positive and life-affirming work in **North**. Here, for a moment, Heaney imagines the impossible: a Viking death which actually breaks the cycle of "scoretaking". In his portrayal of Gunnar Hamundarson who "lay beautiful/inside his burial mound,/though dead by violence/and unavenged", the poet shows the Irish people what might be. The vision quickly passes: Hogni and Skarp-Hedin interpret Gunnar's "verses" as a call to vengeance,[25] Catholic and Protestant continue to murder each other; but the final stanza of *Funeral Rites*, with its potent combination of pagan and Christian resurrection imagery shows, more graphically than *The Tollund Man* could, that peace and freedom are the reward of those who dare to renounce the killing.

Poems of healing: The return to Mossbawn

The "feminine" image upon which Heaney constructed this most positive "masculine" thought of the entire book, is based on that childhood experience of death explored in such early poems as *Mid-Term Break*: from his youthful memories of "stepping in to lift the coffins/of dead relations" in Part I of *Funeral Rites*, grows the epic, national vision of Part III.

Two other works in **North** also inspire hope; and like *Funeral Rites*, both of them draw their strength from the farming world Heaney knew in early life. *Sunlight* and *The Seed Cutters* are poems written "in dedication" to Mossbawn and offered to Mary Heaney, the aunt who helped raise the poet when he was a child. Like *Churning Day* and *Digging* from **Death of a Naturalist**, they present lovingly detailed descriptions of the timeless, ritual activities of the farm. Here once again as in *Funeral Rites*, Heaney is concerned to offer images of healing; but now he does so by taking up a theme suggested in *Servant Boy*: the woman in *Sunlight* and the Seed Cutters are carrying the "warm eggs" of ordinary, decent behaviour which that "jobber among shadows" had protected through "the back-end of a bad year". The values symbolised by those "warm eggs" possess none of the formal, epic qualities of *Funeral Rites*; but perhaps for this very reason they stand a more realistic chance of satisfying strife-torn Ulster's need for "ceremony" and "customary rhythms".

What they do offer is something very easily taken for granted and yet something without which life is infinitely impoverished: that undramatic, daily routine of caring for others which is represented in *Sunlight* by a woman standing "in a floury apron/by the window". Beyond this, the quiet, domestic order of the kitchen and the slow, deliberate, silent work of the seed cutters, provide "a space again" – a blissful sense of release from the violence of Ulster. While life in Londonderry and Belfast rushes at a pace dictated by riot and bomb-blast, the inhabitants of the world of Mossbawn have "time to kill" and are "taking their time", counting the days by the "cooling" of the sun "against the wall/of each long afternoon", relying on clocks merely to measure "the scone rising". Untroubled by time, these people appear themselves to be timeless. "Breughel,/You'll know them if I can get them true", Heaney remarks of the Seed Cutters; and the woman dusting her baking-board "with a goose's wing" in *Sunlight* would have seemed equally familiar to the painter. In *Viking Dublin: Trial Pieces*, the poet sums up the stranglehold which history exerts upon the people of Ulster when he describes himself as "pinioned by ghosts". If only he and they could rediscover the "calendar customs" – the ancient, seasonal round of the Seed Cutters – and exorcise the "ghosts" of sectarian hate, then Protestant and Catholic might at last remove their religious labels and meet each other simply as people, bound together by the fundamental human experience of wresting a living from the earth. Thus might we "compose the frieze/With all of us there, our anonymities".

Like *Funeral Rites*, *Sunlight* and *The Seed Cutters* also provide a note of elegiac consolation. The fact that these images of domestic or agricultural labour have survived Norse invasion or Elizabethan war suggests that "the warm eggs" of civilized behaviour will be carried unbroken through this particular crisis as well. "Balor will die/and Byrthnoth and Sitting Bull"; the "goddess" of *Kinship* will swallow "our love and terror": ultimately, the sorrows of history will disappear and only the natural cycle of generation and death remain. The inevitable triumph of nature over history is powerfully represented in the "Bog Poems", where Heaney describes the gradual transformation of historical figures into "barked sapling", "turf clod" or "black river". In *Sunlight* and *The Seed Cutters*, that triumph is joyfully anticipated by the release of a flood of sensuous images not seen since **Door into the Dark**. The two poems form an oasis of light and warmth between the cold landscapes of **Wintering Out** and **North**, as once again water pours like honey or the "tuck and frill" of leaf-sprout "flowers" like hope itself "on the seed potatoes". "There was a sunlit absence", Heaney writes, searching for a phrase to define what Mossbawn means to him; and yet what is absent here is the noise, the violence, the hatred which is Ireland's historical legacy. In place of the Bog Queen who represents these nihilistic forces, Mossbawn has a different female deity who, like the woman in *The Wife's Tale*, offers images of warmth, fertility, and, above all, love "like a tinsmith's scoop/sunk past its gleam/in the meal-bin." Placed at the start of **North**, *Sunlight* shines like a beacon of hope through the darkness which follows it.

Heaney's return to his poetic roots

Paradoxically, these three optimistic poems owe their existence to the negative impulses which dominate the book as a whole. That sense of despair which stopped Heaney from looking for solutions to the problems of Ireland and caused him to turn in upon himself instead, brought an increased concern with the very nature of poetry writing: in *Gifts of Rain* Heaney had asked questions "for my children's sake"; now he asks them for the sake of his art.

The answers he receives all urge the same course of action: a movement back, at this time of crisis and uncertainty, to the poetic ground he knows best – the landscape of **Death of a Naturalist** and **Door into the Dark**. In *Fosterage*, for example, Michael McLaverty counsels him to adopt that detached but intensely descriptive poetic style so characteristic of his first book, and encourages the young poet "to set the darkness echoing" by sending him out with words "imposing" on his tongue like "obols" – coins which, according to Greek mythology, gain the bearer access to the land of the dead. McLaverty's advice is echoed by the "longship's swimming tongue" in the title poem of **North**, where the exhortations to "Lie down/in the word-hoard", to "Keep your eye clear", and, especially, to "trust the feel of what nubbed treasure/your hands have known", advocate no dramatic new change of poetic direction, but endorse what has gone before.

Nowhere does Heaney follow the advice offered by the Vikings more exactly than in his use of language in **North**. Exhorted to "Lie down/in the word-hoard", he quarries more deeply than ever among the treasuries of Gaelic and Anglo-Saxon – the twin legacies of his divided cultural heritage – excavating such curiousities as "pampooties", "gombeen-men", "pash", "felloes" or "crannog". The process of linguistic exploration brought to fruition here can also be observed at work in **Wintering Out**, but something which is special to **North** is Heaney's response to that final instruction: "trust the feel of what nubbed treasure/your hands have known." Just as a musician might reinterpret an early theme in a later piece of work, so, in this final sequence of the **Selected Poems**, the poet seems to rediscover the images and sensations of his first three books and to redefine them in the light of his now mature experience.

The first part of *Funeral Rites*, for example, recalls *Mid-Term Break*. The earlier poem derives its force from that almost eerie sense of detachment with which Heaney responds to his brother's death. The later work's description of a similar scene, however, is far more compassionate and concerned: the faces of the dead are "Dear soapstone masks" which he wants to kiss; the departure of the funeral cortege wrenches the fabric of his life like a "black glacier ... pushed away"; the corpses' "dough-white hands" are "shackled in rosary beads". Heaney's reworking of his childhood experiences of death here also brings him a more profound understanding and serene acceptance of it. Where *Mid-Term Break* shows how death can shatter a family and force a child to assume adult responsibility too early, *Funeral Rites* offers a more positive alternative view by showing how it can also be absorbed into the pattern of daily life though the controlling process of ritual.

In the latter poem, therefore, the poet focuses on the ceremonial trappings of mourning: the "dulse-brown shroud", the "quilted satin cribs", the "little gleaming crosses" of the coffin "nail-heads". These symbols did not count for much in *Mid-Term Break*, where candles, for example, simply "soothed the bedside" of the corpse; but now, those same candles are granted a far greater significance by Heaney's description of "the flames hovering/to the women hovering". The flames and the women are linked by a shared verb here to signify just how precisely the candles express the common grief of the mourners who have, consequently, no need for the "crying" and "tearless sighs" of the earlier poem. The sense of perfectly controlled, perfectly expressed emotion found in *Funeral Rites* gives that work a dignity, calm and inner strength which contrasts sharply with the angry bewilderment of *Mid-Term Break*, and which enables the poet, who before felt "embarrassed" in the presence of death, to play his part in the ceremony with equanimity: "I knelt courteously/admiring it all".

Throughout **North**, images from previous books are reworked and brought to fruition. Sometimes, the whole later poem offers a literal fulfilment of the earlier work. In *Shoreline*, for example, Heaney stood upon the "hissing" strands of Ireland and watched for "A black hawk bent on the sail" of a Viking long-boat – in *North* he returns to "the hammered shod of a bay" where that "longship's swimming tongue" speaks to him. Sometimes it is a single image which is refined or reshaped. Thus the eels portrayed in *A Lough Neagh Sequence* emerge again in the poet's description of the Graubelle Man's spine, or of the "line" carved in Part I of *Viking Dublin: Trial Pieces*. Whatever form the process of reworking takes, it follows the same pattern of movement. Detachment gives way to involvement; personal concern for the immediate family or the natural world broadens to include an awareness of history and society. The biological father of *Follower* makes way for the "Old fathers" of *Viking Dublin*; the "door into the dark" which once led into a blacksmith's forge, becomes the "dark/elderberry place" of an ancient sacrificial victim who symbolizes a nation's sufferings.

The process of reworking described here achieves its most complete expression in *Kinship*, where Heaney conducts a masterly reappraisal of his response to the Irish bog from **Death of a Naturalist** to **North**. Each section of the poem explores a different stage of his creative journey. In Part I he steps back "through origins" to search again for those twin sensations of love and awe which the bog itself first inspired in him when, as a small boy, he "bathed in a moss-hole". This is the landscape of *Personal Helicon* and *Bogland*; and, as though to acknowledge the fact, the last two stanzas of Part I actually echo the language of these earlier poems. In the first stanza of Part II, Heaney concludes the childhood phase of his journey by recalling that sense of the bog as a place of retribution first expressed in *Death of a Naturalist*. Once again, tribute is paid to the earlier poem when the poet's reference to "the slime kingdoms" brings to mind the "great slime kings" who once ruled there. With a gesture to *Anahorish* and *Broagh*, Heaney considers the meaning of the word "bog" itself, and pursues it through its several progressively dark and complex manifestations from treasure-house of history in Part II to domain of the "Nerthus" or Bog Queen in Part III. "This centre holds/and spreads", the poet writes at the start of Part IV as the abiding, stablizing image of his poetry yields up its last secret: the myth of the Tollund Man Part V and, finally in Part VI, of his fiercer counterparts from **North** itself.

Summary and conclusion

When **North** was published in 1975, many critics endorsed the publishers' view that the poems of Heaney's fourth book were "more varied in range and subject matter, than any of his previous collections."[26] In fact, **Wintering Out** is a far more innovative work. Apart from its broader historical perspective, its introspection and the fact that all its themes cohere round the social and political implications of being "north", the volume simply refines the preoccupations, images and techniques of the previous book. The same interplay of "masculine" and "feminine" poetic modes can be observed; austere, concentrated verse structures create the same effect of tunnelling or intense meditation; the relationship between "locale" and "utterance" is examined again; the same "befitting emblems of adversity" explore the poet's sense of divided loyalty and his fatalistic vision of history. For all these reasons, and because it returns to the starting-point of Heaney's artistic journey, **North** should be regarded as a work of consolidation and completion, rather than as a work of innovation: it represents the ending of one phase of his creative life, not the beginning of a new one.

That Heaney himself felt about **North** in this way is made clear by his description of it as "the book all books were leading to";[27] and his sense of finality is enhanced in *Exposure*, the final poem of the volume where, instead of finding the "meteorite" of new inspiration, the poet portrays himself as one who must make do with what is old, familiar, even exhausted: "I walk through damp leaves,/Husks, the spent flukes of autumn".

What more was there for him to say about the themes which had preoccupied his poetic career so far? **North** had pursued the "Irish myth" to its extremity. When there were no further "emblems of adversity" to explore, the poet had turned instead to an examination of his own conscience, analysing with fierce honesty the whole range of his thoughts on the Ulster crisis, irrespective of the criticism such confessional poetry might provoke. It is no wonder, then, that in *Kinship*, the poem which reviews all that Heaney had so far tried to do, he should put so many of his responses in the past tense – most significant of all, that comment towards the end of Part IV: "I grew out of all this".

Bogland, Ulster, the Irish myth, had been written out. The luxuriant verse forms and extended metaphors of **Death of a Naturalist** had been pruned back as far as they could go. If Heaney was not to spend the rest of his artistic life reworking and refining the thoughts, images and structures of his earlier books, then Glanmore, County Wicklow, would have to provide a new start. **North** is not it. Significantly, the final work in the collection, the final work in the **Selected Poems**, shows the poet looking back, not forward. Isolated in a landscape that is creatively as well as physically wintry, he asks, "How did I end up like this?" The **Selected Poems** provide the answer.

Notes and References

1. In 1974, Heaney published **Stations**, a collection of twenty-one short prose paragraph pieces based on his experience of childhood. None of these works were included in the **Selected Poems**.
2. The only poem in **Wintering Out** to deal explicitly with the troubles of Ulster is an introductory piece, which stands outside the main body of the work. In **North**, this same poem re-emerges as Part IV of *Whatever You Say Say Nothing*.
3. Seamus Deane, *Unhappy and at Home* Heaney interview, **The Crane Bag**, I,I, 1977, p. 66.
4. **North**, pp. 60, 58, 70, 57, 68, 69.
5. *Unhappy and at Home*, **The Crane Bag** p. 66.
6. *Out of London: Ulster's Troubles*, p. 23.
7. Heaney, **Poetry Book Society Bulletin**, 85 (Summer 1975), p. 1.
8. **North**, p. 57.
9. Heaney, **Poetry Book Society Bulletin**, p. 1.
10. **North**, pp. 56, 58, 59, 69.
11. Ibid., p. 60.
12. *Mother Ireland*, p. 790.
13. W.B. Yeats, *The Second Coming*
14. *Feeling into Words*, p. 59.
15. John Keats, *Ode to a Nightingale*.
16. **North**, p. 58.
17. *Feeling into Words*, p. 57.
18. *The Fire i' the Flint*, p. 87.
19. **North**, p. 59.
20. *Mother Ireland*, p. 790.
21. William Shakespeare, **King Richard II**, Act II, Scene i, 11. 156, 155.
22. See for example Ciaran Carson, *Escaped from the Massacre?*
23. *The Fire i' the Flint*, pp. 95–6.
24. *The Sense of Place*, pp. 142–3.
25. The scene which inspired this section of *Funeral Rites* occurs in chapter 78 of **Njal's Saga**, Translated by Magnus Magnusson and Hermann Palsson, London: Penguin, 1960.
26. Quoted on the cover of the first edition of **North**.
27. Heaney, **Rambles in Ireland** interview, p. 169.

Glossary to 'The Selected Poems'

The linguistic origin of each word is indicated by a letter placed in brackets at the end of the definition.

KEY

E	= English	L	= Latin
F	= French	S	= Scottish
G	= German	Sc.	= Scandinavian
I	= Irish		

Althing ('North') — Viking assembly or parliament. (Sc.)

Bawn ('A New Song') — Either: "white" from the Irish *bán*. Or: a fortified enclosure, from the Anglicized version of the Irish word *bábhun*.

Bullaun ('A New Song') — A hollow scooped out of a boulder for grinding purposes, usually found at early monastic sites. (I.)

Cairn ('Kinship') — A monument of stones raised in a pyramid shape. (I.)

Chanter ('Gifts of Rain') — The finger-pipe of a bag-pipe. (F.)

Crannog ('Kinship') — A raised structure, usually made of wood. (I.)

Dander ('The Other Side') — To stroll or saunter. (S.)

Demesne ('A New Song') — An estate, such as the land attached to a mansion. (F.)

Felloes ('Kinship')	Curved pieces of wood which, joined together, form a wheel rim. (G.)
Flax ('Death of a Naturalist')	Plant grown for making linen. (G.)
Gombeen Men ('Viking Dublin')	Money-lenders. (I.)
Haggard ('Servant Boy')	Stackyard (Sc.)
Haggers ('Viking Dublin')	Cutters (with swords, etc.) (Sc.)
Monstrance ('The Last Mummer')	An ornamental sacred vessel used for displaying the host in Christian religious services. (L.)
Mossland ('Traditions')	Bogland. (E.)
Pampooties ('Viking Dublin')	Leather sandals used in the Aran Islands. (I.)
Rath ('A New Song')	An enclosure, usually ring-shaped and bordered by a bank and ditch. (I.)
Rigs ('Broagh')	Ridges. (E.)
Rosary ('The Other Side')	Catholic prayer beads. 165 beads are divided on a string into 15 sets. (L.)
Souterrain ('Hercules and Antaeus')	A series of underground chambers. (F.)
Staple ('Thatcher')	A short "u" shaped rod for holding something in place. (G.)
Stigmata ('Westering')	Marks resembling the wounds of the crucified Christ. (L.)

Historical notes to the selected poems

At a Potato Digging

Part III of the poem refers to the Great Potato Famine which afflicted Ireland between 1845 and 1849. Before the famine, the population of the country had reached eight million, and the potato was the staple food for almost half that number. The crop partially failed in the autumn of 1845, but it was the total failure which followed in subsequent years which sealed the fate of the peasantry. In 1847 alone, nearly 250,000 people died of starvation or fever, and 200,000 emigrated to America. Between 1845 and 1849, over one million people were lost through death or emigration. By 1871, the population had fallen to five and a half million. The British Government's refusal to intervene until 1847 served to increase the resentment of the Irish Catholics, while wide-scale emigration to America helped establish large anti-British concentrations of Irish people in the United States.

Shoreline

The "chinking Normans" first invaded Ireland in 1171, when King Henry II of England brought over an army to support the claim of his fellow countryman, Richard de Clare, (known as "Strongbow") to the throne of the Kingdom of Leinster. Although Henry himself was content to receive the homage of the Irish chieftains and then return to England, many of his Norman companions in arms pushed on into Irish territory, winning land for themselves by force. By 1300, almost two thirds of the country was under Norman control. Like other invaders before them, the Normans gradually absorbed the culture and language of the natives, becoming "more Irish than the Irish themselves".

Requiem for the Croppies

The poem refers to the Irish uprisings of 1798 which occurred in Antrim, Down, North Leinster, Wicklow and, particularly, Wexford. Inspired by the republican ideals of revolutionary France and the non-sectarian leadership of the United Irishmen, and angered by the rents and tithes which they were forced to pay to the Anglo-Protestant landlords and church, the Catholic peasantry of Wexford rose in rebellion.

The flashpoint occurred on the night of Saturday, 26th May 1798, when British soldiers burned the church and home of Father John Murphy of Boleyvogue, together with some twenty neighbouring farmhouses. After initial military successes, including the capture of the town of Enniscorthy, Murphy and his followers were almost surrounded by the English forces under Generals Lake and Johnson on 9th June at Vinegar Hill, to the east of the town. Outnumbered by 20,000 to some 7,000, undisciplined and armed with little more than pikes and farmyard implements, the rebels withstood overwhelming fire for several hours before escaping through the last remaining gap in the enemy lines.

Atrocities were committed on both sides, and the rebellion was put down with particular savagery, because its combination of Catholic nationalism and revolutionary politics seemed to pose a new and dangerous threat to Anglo-protestant control of Ireland. The rebel "Croppies" were so called because they cut their hair short, in the manner of the French revolutionaries.

Bog Oak

The figures described by the famous Elizabethan Protestant poet and English settler Edmund Spenser here are native Irish victims of the Munster rebellion against the forces of Queen Elizabeth's England.

The rebellion began in 1569 when James FitzMaurice FitzGerald, cousin and adviser to the Earl of Desmond, organized a Catholic crusade against the Protestant forces of the crown which, since the reign of Henry VIII, had played an increasingly dominant part in Irish affairs. Defeated by Sir John Perrot in 1572, FitzMaurice escaped to the Continent in 1575, where he raised an army with the help of the Pope and the Catholic King of Spain, who saw the rebellion as an opportunity to threaten Protestant England through her "back door".

In 1579, FitzMaurice landed at Dingle on the Kerry coast with 300 Spanish and Italian troops. A year later, this army was reinforced by an additional 600 Spanish soldiers who occupied a fort at Smerwick, some eight miles north west of Dingle. After a three day seige beginning on 7th November 1580, the Spaniards surrendered to Lord Grey de Wilton, who put them to death. The war continued for another three years, during which time almost all of Munster was laid waste. FitzMaurice himself was killed in a skirmish soon after landing, but the rebellion finally petered out in November 1583, following the death of the Earl of Desmond.

Spenser, who approved of such actions as the Smerwick massacre, gained Kilcolman castle and 3,028 acres of land in County Cork confiscated from the Desmonds after the conflict. In October 1598, however, Kilcolman was burned down by supporters of another rebellious Irish chieftain, Hugh O'Neill. It is said that Spenser's infant son died in the blaze. Having lost his possessions, Spenser returned to London where he died the following year.

The Last Mummer

The Mummers of Lough Erne would boat round the islands of the lake at Christmas time, performing their mumming play in shops and houses in return for money and drink. The mummer's costume consisted of a pair of old trousers tied around the knee with straw, and a potato sack for a shirt. On his head, the mummer wore a great conical helmet made of straw which was so heavy that he had to walk with small sideways steps in order to balance it. The mummers would enter a house in single file, the first man in being known as the "hero". As they walked, they played music on their fiddles and melodeons.

The mumming play was a loose mixture of Christian imagery and pagan resurrection myth. St. George was killed, only to be raised back to life miraculously in order to vanquish evil in the form of Beelzebub. It is said that the play symbolised the death of the old year at midwinter and the birth of the new. A visit from the mummers ensured good luck for the year ahead. As they entered a house, they would say the following rhyme:

> Here I come with my poems and rhymes
> To put you in mind of the Christmas times.
> It was neither money, home or want which brought me here.
> But to put you in mind of a happy New Year.

The Other Side

The sense of alienation between the Catholic and Protestant farmers described in this poem can be attributed, ultimately, to the "plantation" policy operated by the British state in the 16th and 17th Centuries.

The plantation system began under Queen Mary Tudor and was continued by Elizabeth, James I and Oliver Cromwell. The aim was to extend English control over Ireland by confiscating the estates of rebellious Anglo-Irish lords or native chieftains and offering them to "undertakers" who would then "plant" the land with British families loyal to the Crown.

The plantation of Ulster began after the flight from Ireland of the rebel Earls of Tyrone and Tyrconnell in September 1607. Declaring their estates forfeit, the Crown distributed large areas of Armagh, Cavan, Derry, Donegal, Fermanagh and Tyrone to settlers from England and, particularly, lowland Scotland. The Scots flavour to the speech of the Protestant farmer described in *The Other Side* ("kirk", "dandering") suggests that his ancestors belonged to this latter group. By 1628, there were 2,000 British families in the six "planted" counties of Ulster. In 1652, the Cromwellian "Long" Parliament's "Act for the Settlement of Ireland" set the seal on the plantation policy. From that date onwards, the majority of landlords in Ireland were Protestant rather than Catholic.

The plantations of Ireland formed just one strand in the general pattern of British overseas expansion which began in the 16th Century. The Elizabethan adventurer, Sir Walter Raleigh, for example, established colonies in Ireland and America. The concept of Ireland as a colony of England, and Raleigh's particular part in the colonisation process, are of especial interest to Seamus Heaney. Had plantation not taken place, many of the religious and political problems currently besetting Ulster would not exist.

The Tollund Man

The body of the Tollund Man was discovered preserved in the peat at Tollund in Jutland, Denmark, on 8th May 1950. Research has dated the body to the Early Iron Age, about two thousand years ago. The Tollund Man was found naked except for a cap and belt. A noose had been placed round his neck and he had been strangled, probably as a sacrifice to Nerthus, the Earth Goddess of the Germanic tribes. The body of the Tollund Man can be seen at the Silkeborg Museum, Central Jutland. Heaney did not fulfil his vow to visit it till 1973.

Funeral Rites

The "great chambers of Boyne" make up the large prehistoric necropolis of **Brugh na Boinne**, which can be found three miles south east of Slane, County Meath, between the Slane/Drogheda road and the great loop of the River Boyne.

The main features of the site are the cairn of Knowth (280 feet in diameter, 40/50 feet high) and, three quarters of a mile to the south east, the famous chambered cairn of Newgrange (280 feet in diameter, 44 feet high). The body of the mound at Newgrange is secured by a retaining kerb of giant stones, eight to ten feet long, decorated with spiral, lozenge or zig-zag motifs. A 62 feet long passage leads to a cruciform burial chamber. One and three quarter miles north east of Newgrange lies the chambered cairn of Dowth (280 feet in diameter, 47 feet high). The passage to the burial chamber here is 27 feet long. Beside the three great cairns, **Brugh na Boinne** also contains many tumuli, raised mounds, embankments and standing stones.

Brugh na Boinne was established as a spiritual centre in the New Stone Age or "Neolithic" period (circa 3,000 BC). It equals Stonehenge and Avebury in importance.

Shoreline, North, Viking Dublin: Trial pieces

The Vikings who first raided and then settled in Ireland came from Norway. Their raids began with an attack on Lambay island in 795, and increased in intensity over the next twelve years. By 830, the raiders had become settlers, with the Norwegians dominating most of the east and west coasts of Ireland. In 839, the Viking Turgeis declared himself "King of all foreigners in Erin" and, two years later, founded a harbour-fort on the River Liffey at the "Black Pool" (Irish: *Duibhlinn*, Norse: *Dyfflin*) which was to become the city of Dublin.

For the next eighty years, Irish and Norwegians struggled for supremacy, with the latter gaining mastery over much of Ireland after the battles of Confrey in 916 and Climashogue in 919. The Norwegian attempt at conquest was finally thwarted at the battle of Clontarf in 1014, where Brian Boru, *árd rí* or "High King" of Ireland, defeated the invaders at the cost of his own life. Gradually, the "Ostmen" or "Easterners" intermarried with the Irish and accepted Christianity.

The impact of the Vikings upon Ireland should not be regarded as merely destructive. Their presence enriched the native culture both artistically and commercially. The Vikings founded the country's first cities at Dublin, Wexford, Waterford, Cork and Limerick, and these became centres of trade from which Norwegian longships carried Irish hides and wool to Europe, bringing back wine and slaves. One early 11th Century King of Norse Dublin, Sigtryggr Silkenbeard, was the first ruler in Ireland to mint a coinage.

Bog Queen

The body of this woman was discovered as early as the spring of 1781, not in Denmark, but in a peat bog on Drumkeragh Mountain, County Down, Ireland. The peat-cutter who found the body reburied it, but not before many of the numerous garments discovered with the corpse had been removed by visitors. The wife of a local land-owner, Lady Moira, recorded the find and paid a large amount of money for a lock of hair and some fine pieces of green and red cloth belonging to the dead woman. Most notable among the possessions found in the grave were a veil, a diadem, three woollen rugs, a skirt and an elaborate cape probably brought from the East by Phoenician traders.

The Grauballe Man

The naked body of the Grauballe Man was discovered in Nebelgard Fen, eleven miles from Tollund, on 26th April 1952. He was probably thirty years old, and died sometime between 210 and 410 AD. His throat had been slashed, and he was possibly killed as a midwinter sacrifice. The Grauballe Man can be seen at the Museum of Prehistory just outside Aarhus.

Punishment, Strange Fruit

The subject of these two poems is the so-called "Windeby Girl", whose preserved body was discovered nearly two years after that of the Tollund Man in Domland Fen south of Eckernförde in Schleswig, Denmark. This young girl (she was aged about fourteen) had been stripped almost naked, shaved, blindfolded and drowned under twenty inches of water in a peat bog. The body had been held in place by a stone and birch branches.

The Roman historian Tacitus observed that the Germanic tribes would shave the heads of adulterous women, scourge them, and drive them out of the village. It has been conjectured that the Windeby Girl was drowned for adultery. She probably died in the first century AD. Her body was taken to the County Museum in Schleswig.

The Politics of Northern Ireland

Direct Rule

The Government of Ireland Act passed in 1920 gave England ultimate sovereignty over Ulster. In March 1972, English Prime Minister Edward Heath invoked the act to take responsibility for law and order from the Stormont Government. When Stormont refused to agree, Heath suspended it. Since then, Ulster has been ruled directly from Westminster by a Secretary of State for Northern Ireland.

Fenians

An organization of political activists, composed mainly of Irish-Americans who, in the 1850s, banded together to work for Irish independence. The Fenians were prepared to use violence to achieve their aims.

Fianna Fail

"Soldiers of Destiny". This party was formed in 1926 by Eamon de Valera in order to mount a political challenge to the Free State Government, *Cumann na nGaedheal*. Fianna Fail came to power after the general election of 1932.

Fine Gael

Otherwise known as the United Ireland Party. Fine Gael was founded by William Cosgrave after the defeat of the *Cumann na nGaedheal* government in 1932. The party consisted largely of supporters of the Free State. It came to power under John Costello in 1948. It was Costello's coalition government which declared the Free State a republic on Easter Monday 1949.

Gerrymandering

The adjusting of electoral boundaries to give one party an unfair advantage. Gerrymandering was one of the main grievances of the Catholic Civil Rights Movement in the late 1960s.

Internment

The imprisonment of suspects without trial under a "Special Powers Act". The introduction of internment by the Stormont Government in August 1971 was meant to curb the activities of the I.R.A., but actually inflamed Catholic opinion and lead to an escalation of the violence.

Irish Republican Army (IRA)

Volunteers raised to fight for an independent Ireland in 1914. In 1916 they were reorganized and renamed as the Irish Republican Army. Their aim was to use force to end the partition of Ireland established by the treaty of 1921. In the 1930s the I.R.A. became more socialist in its politics, and in 1969 the organization split between the "Officials" who wished to campaign for a socialist Ireland, and the "Provisionals" whose priority remained the ending of Partition by armed struggle.

Northern Ireland

Established as a political unit by the Government of Ireland Act of 1920. The state of Northern Ireland is made up of six of the nine counties which formed the historic province of Ulster. The six counties are: Antrim, Armagh, Derry, Down, Fermanagh and Tyrone. The three counties which were made part of the Free State are Cavan, Donegal and Monaghan. The state of Northern Ireland comprised the largest area which would give a workable Protestant majority in a Northern Irish Parliament. Cavan, Donegal and Monaghan were excluded because their populations were predominantly Catholic.

Orange Order

An organization founded in 1795 to protect Protestant interests. Its main concern was to prevent Catholics from buying land in Protestant areas. The Orange Order exerts a large influence over the Unionist Party. Its members march on 12th July to celebrate the triumph of Protestantism in Ireland which followed the defeat of the Catholic James II by the forces of William of Orange at the Battle of the Boyne on 1st July 1690.

Partition

The division of Ireland established by the Government of Ireland Act in 1920. The country was divided into a twenty-six county Catholic Free State, and a six county Protestant Ulster.

Royal Ulster Constabulary (RUC)

Established as an armed force in 1922 to police the new state of Northern Ireland. One third of the RUC were supposed to be Catholic. In fact, most are members of the Orange Order.

Social Democratic and Labour Party (SDLP)

Northern Irish Catholic opposition party, pledged to defend Catholic interests by constitutional means.

Sinn Fein

"We Ourselves". The party was founded in 1905 by Arthur Griffith. In 1917 it emerged as the political wing of the revolutionary movement for Irish independence when Eamon de Valera became its leader. In 1926, de Valera left the party to found Fianna Fail. Sinn Fein remained the political wing of the IRA.

Stormont

The seat of the Parliament and Government of Northern Ireland from 1921 to 1972. Stormont is situated four and a half miles east of Belfast.

Ulster Defence Association (UDA)

A para-military force founded in 1972 to defend Protestant areas from the IRA.

Unionist Party

The Ulster Unionist Council was formed in 1905 to preserve the union with Britain. In 1921, the Council became the Unionist Party. Pledged to defend Protestant and Orange interests, it won every Ulster election between 1921 and 1972. Its leader, Sir James Craig, was the first Prime Minister of Stormont. He held office from 1921 to 1940.

Political events since 1914: A Glossary

1914		Beginning of World War 1. John Redmond, leader of Irish Home Rule party, pledged support for Britain, but some Irish nationalists disagreed.
1916		Easter Rising of Irish republicans of Dublin.
1919		Republican Government established in Ireland.
1920		War between the Republican and British forces. The British "Government of Ireland Act" established partition by dividing the country into "Northern Ireland" (Six Counties) and "Southern Ireland" (Twenty-six Counties).
1921	6th December	The Anglo-Irish Treaty signed in London, by which Southern Ireland accepted "Government of Ireland Act", conceded dominion status and became known as the Irish Free State.
1922–3		Civil War between Republican and Irish Free State forces.
1925		Boundary Commission Report kept existing partition.
1932		Economic warfare between Britain and Irish Free State. De Valera became Prime Minister of Ireland.
1937		New Constitution for Free State, which became an independent state but remained in the Commonwealth.
1939		World War II. Southern Ireland declared herself neutral. Ulster supported Britain.
1948		Republic of Ireland Act severed last constitutional links with Britain.
1956		I.R.A. activity in North and South.
1968	5th October	Civil Rights demonstration in Londonderry broken up by police with some violence.
1969	4th January	People's Democracy March attacked at Burntollet Bridge outside Londonderry.
	12th–14th August	Serious rioting in Belfast and Londonderry.
	13th August	British troops brought into Northern Ireland.
1971	July	Opposition parties withdrew from Stormont, (the Parliament of Northern Ireland).
	August	Internment introduced.
1972	30th January	"Bloody Sunday". Thirteen people killed by British troops following the illegal march from Londonderry.
	24th March	Stormont ended. Direct Rule begins.
1973	March	Plebiscite held on the border – boycotted by Catholic parties.

	June	Election for new Assembly to replace Stormont.
	December	Council of Ireland established by the U.K. Government, Northern Ireland Executive (designate) and Irish Government.
1974	January	Power-sharing Executive set up.
	February	U.K. General Election and 11 out of 12 seats were won by candidates opposed to the Executive.
	May	Following strike action initiated by Ulster Workers' Council the Executive resign. Direct Rule resumed.
1975	May	Constitutional Convention established to put forward recommendations on the future of Northern Ireland.
1976	March	Constitutional Convention dissolved following its failure to produce a unanimous report, and the rejection of the report by the U.K. Government.
	August	Formation of the Peace Movement.
1977	May	10 day strike by Ulster Unionist Action Council for tougher action against the I.R.A. and in support of the report of the Constitutional Convention.
1979	March	Number of Parliamentary constituencies increase to 17.
1981	October	End of seven month hunger strike protest against conditions in the Maze Prison – 10 died.
	November	Anglo-Irish Intergovernmental Council created to discuss matters of mutual concern.
1982	October	Election of the new Assembly. First meeting boycotted by the Social Democratic and Labour Party and Sinn Fein.
1983		Gerry Fitt, S.D.L.P. member, defeated by Gerry Adams, Provisional Sinn Fein leader, in the General Election.
1984	May	New Ireland Forum report published by the political parties of the Republic and the S.D.L.P.
	October	I.R.A. bomb at the Grand Hotel, Brighton.
1985	November	Anglo-Irish Agreement signed to set up an Intergovernmental Conference.
1986	March	One day strike organized by Unionist Leaders against the Anglo-Irish Agreement.

Suggestions for further reading

Books about Heaney's poetry

Broadbridge, Edward (ed.). **Seamus Heaney.** Copenhagen: Danmarks Radio, 1977.

Buttel, Robert. **Seamus Heaney.** Lewisburg, Pa.: Bucknell University Press, 1975.

Curtis, Tony (ed.). **The Art of Seamus Heaney.** Cardiff: Poetry Wales Press, 1985.

Morrison, Blake. **Seamus Heaney** (Contemporary Writers.) London and New York: Methuen, 1982.

Books and essays by Seamus Heaney

Some Books and essays not included in the **Selected Poems** or **Preoccupations (1980).**

Stations. Belfast: Ulsterman Publications, 1975.

Robert Lowell: A Memorial Address and Elegy. London and Boston, Mass.: Faber, 1978.

Gravities. Newcastle: Charlotte Press, 1979. (With drawings by Noel Connor.)

Field Work. London and Boston, Mass.: Faber, 1979.

An Open Letter. Derry: Field Day Theatre Pamphlets, 1983.

"Among Schoolchildren": A John Malone Memorial Lecture. Belfast: University Press, 1984.

Station Island. London and Boston, Mass.: Faber, 1984.

Sweeney Astray. London and Boston, Mass.: Faber, 1984.

Hailstones. Dublin: Gallery Press, 1985.

Field Work and **Station Island** are full-length collections of poetry. **Sweeney Astray** is a verse translation of an epic Irish poem.

Seamus Heaney: Reference Works

Pearson, Henry. **Seamus Heaney: A Bibliographical Checklist. American Book Collector**, III, March/April, 1982, pp. 31–42.

The books on Heaney by Curtis and Morrison also contain excellent bibliographies.

Books on the history of Ireland

General

Beckett, J.C. **A Short History of Ireland**. London: Hutchinson, 1984.

Kee, Robert. **Ireland: A History**. London: Little, 1982.

O'Brien, Máire and Conor Cruise. **A Concise History of Ireland**. London: Thames and Hudson, 1972.

Prehistoric

Evans, E.E. **Prehistoric and Early Christian Ireland**. London: Batsford, 1966.

Celtic

Glob. P.V. **The Bog People**. London: Faber, 1969.

MacNeill, Eoinn. **Celtic Ireland**. Dublin: University Press, 1981.

Ross, Anne. **Pagan Celtic Britain: Studies in Iconography and Tradition**. London: Routledge and Kegan Paul, 1967.

Norse

Bradley, John. **Viking Dublin Exposed**. Dublin: O'Brien Press, 1984.

Brøndsted, Johannes. **The Vikings**. London: Pelican, 1960.

Curriculum Development Unit (ed.). **Viking Settlement to Medieval Dublin**. Dublin: O'Brien Press, 1979.

Magnusson, Magnus. **Vikings**. London: Bodley Head, 1980.

Norman

Otway-Ruthven, A.J. **A History of Medieval Ireland**. London: St. Martin Press, 1968.

Sheehy, Maurice. **When the Normans Came to Ireland**. Cork: Mercier Press, 1975.

Elizabethan

Henley, Pauline. **Spenser in Ireland**. London: Russell, 1969.

Morton, R.G. **Elizabethan Ireland**. London: Longman, 1971.

Myers (Jr.), James P. (ed.). **A Selection of Writings by Elizabethan Writers on Ireland**. Hamden, Cn.: Archon Books, 1983.

Eighteenth Century (The Rebellion of 1798)

O'Connell, M.R. **Irish Politics and Social Conflict in the Age of the American Revolution**. London: Greenwood Press, 1976.

Nineteenth Century (The Potato Famine)

Woodham-Smith, C. **The Great Hunger**. London: Dutton, 1980.

The Public Record Office of Northern Ireland in Belfast produces an Education Facsimile Series covering the documents of the 1798 Rebellion and the Potato Famine.

Books About Northern Ireland

Darby, John (ed.). **Northern Ireland: The Background to the Conflict**. New York: The University of Syracuse Press, 1983.

Deutsch, Richard R. **Northern Ireland, Nineteen Twenty-One to Nineteen Seventy-Four: A Select Bibliography**. London: The Garland Press, 1974.

Deutsch, Richard R. **Northern Ireland 1968–1974: A Chronology of Events**. Belfast: Blackstaff Press, 1975.

Flackes, W.D. **Northern Ireland: A Political Directory 1968–79**. London: B.B.C. Publications, 1980.

Holland, Jack. **Too Long a Sacrifice: Life and Death in Northern Ireland Since 1969**. London: Penguin, 1982.

Otway Woodward, G.W. **Divided Island** (Studies in 20th Century History.) Auckland: Heinemann Educational Books, 1976.